SACRED ACTS, HOLY CHANGE

Also by Eric H. F. Law,
published by Chalice Press

The Wolf Shall Dwell with the Lamb

The Bush Was Blazing But Not Consumed

Inclusion

SACRED ACTS, HOLY CHANGE

Faithful Diversity and Practical Transformation

ERIC H. F. LAW

CHALICE
PRESS

ST. LOUIS, MISSOURI

Biblical quotations, unless otherwise noted, are from the *New Revised Standard Version Bible*, copyright 1989, Division of Christian Education of the National Council of the Churches of Christ in the United States of America. Used by permission. All rights reserved.

Cover design: Mike Foley
Interior design: Elizabeth Wright
Art direction: Michael Domínguez

This book is printed on acid-free, recycled paper.

Visit Chalice Press on the World Wide Web at
www.chalicepress.com

10 9 8 7 6 5 4 3 2   03 04 05 06

Library of Congress Cataloging–in–Publication Data

Law, Eric H. F.
    Sacred acts, holy change / Eric H. F. Law.
      p.   cm.
    ISBN 0-8272-3452-X (alk. paper)
    1. Church management. 2. Multiculturalism—Religious aspects—Christianity.
I. Title.
BV652 .L36 2001
254—dc21   2001004598

Printed in the United States of America

For Steve Rutberg,
who has shown me that change is never easy,
but with commitment and devotion,
creative transformation can happen.

Contents

Acknowledgments

The wisdom and spirit of this book came from many people: some had come before me, some had been great teachers, some had been nurturers, some were keepers of the vision, and some had been fellow learners. I thank especially Elizabeth Ann High and Walter Loesel for introducing me to their version of the Process for Planned Change. I am grateful for Beverly Shamana (now the bishop of the California-Nevada Annual Conference of the United Methodist Church) and Don Bommarito (now the northeast region director of Percept Group, Inc.) for trusting me enough to let me test this evolving process with the committees and commissions in the California-Pacific Annual Conference while they were associate council directors during the early 1990s. I especially thank Catherine Roskam, the Suffragan Bishop of the Episcopal Diocese of New York for challenging me to design this program and to name it the Kaleidoscope Project. I thank David and Paula Severe for treating me as part of their family whenever I was in Oklahoma in the last two years to facilitate the Kaleidoscope Project. I am forever indebted to the members of the Kaleidoscope Training Teams, which helped me implement, coordinate, and evaluate this process over the years.

In the Episcopal Diocese of New York: Ann Post, Filomena Servellon, Dolores Thompson, William Cruse, Keith McKenna, Ricardo Turcios, and Tamara Banford.

In the Anglican Diocese of New Westminster: Elizabeth Beale, Paul Borthistle, Cathy Derksen, Margaret Derrick, Sheila Flynn, Lois Godfrey, Pat Horrobin, Hyacinth Lawrence, Carla McGhie, Gail McMynn, Michael Prior, Anne Schreck, Jeanette Scott, Carol Simpson, Edgar Tuffin, and Margeurite Verbeek.

In the Oklahoma Annual Conference of the United Methodist Church: David Severe, Janelle Brammer, David Croninger, Karen Howard, Sarah Miller, Fred Sordahl, Mark Watson, and Larry Wilson.

Of course, I must thank all the congregation teams that have participated in the Kaleidoscope Projects in the last five years. I thank them for their commitment and perseverance in searching for ways to faithfully transform their church communities. Finally, I thank Kent Steinbrenner for correcting my grammar and giving excellent suggestions for the first draft of this book.

Introduction

In 1985, while I was serving as the Episcopal campus minister at the University of Southern California, the Diocese of Los Angeles recruited me to be trained as part of a team of congregation consultants who were skilled in helping local churches to move through transition time. Under the leadership of Elizabeth Ann High, a diocesan staff member, and the Reverend Walter Loesel, the chair of the Christian Education and Leadership Training Committee, I was introduced to the iceberg analogy of church organization and a change model called "A Process for Planned Change."

The iceberg analogy was a very helpful tool, not only for understanding organizational change. With my research in cultural anthropology, I have utilized it extensively in my writing and presentation on multicultural organization development and building inclusive community. (See chapters 4 and 5 for a detailed discussion of the iceberg analogy and its application in the change model.)

However, the Process for Planned Change in its original form was not as effective as I would have liked it to be in the places where I applied it. Something was missing in the form of the model that I was taught. Yet, I knew this model had great potential. Therefore, I kept applying this process, modifying it each time based on learning from the last evaluation. Using the theories, theology, and skills that I have developed for building inclusive community over the years, I expanded different parts of the model. I also added new components to it. The most important addition was the centrality of theological reflection in the form of Bible study and the drawing of the outer parameters of the change project.

It was like finding the outer rim (parameters) and the hub (theological reflection) of the wheel. When these essential parts came together, the Process for Planned Change came alive, and it moved like a wheel, effecting faithful movement and change in organizations that worked with it. (See chapter 8 and Figure 8.1 to see the graphic representation of the Process for Planned Change.)

In 1996, after I had done numerous training workshops in multicultural ministry, many of my colleagues who knew and appreciated my work asked me, "What's the next step?" Many said, "When we returned to our home community with our new awareness and skills, we had to deal with enabling our church organizations to change. How do we do that?" At the invitation of Bishop Catherine Roskam of the Episcopal Diocese of New York to address precisely these questions, I designed a program combining training in building inclusive community and the ever-evolving Process for Planned Change. We invited 10 congregation teams to covenant with us for five full days of training in a period of six months. The training would include theory and practice in building inclusive community and moving through the Process for Planned Change, resulting in an action plan that each congregation would take back to implement in order to facilitate the necessary change. The image I use to describe the design is a double helix, like that of a DNA, which is made of two spirals intertwining. One spiral is the Process for Planned Change and the other is the inclusive community skill training. At the center of the training program is regular theological reflection in the form of Bible study and worship. For example, each seven-hour training day is organized like an elongated communion service. In the morning, we would sing hymns and pray together. Then we read scripture together and reflected on it in small groups. Sometimes we would have an individual proclaiming the gospel during the lunch period. Later on in the afternoon, after training and planning workshops, we came together to pray and ask God for guidance and support. Then we ended the day with sharing the body and blood of Christ in the celebration of holy communion. Upon later deliberation, we discovered that the theological reflection was what drove the double helix forward toward transformation and change.

Bishop Roskam named the program the "Kaleidoscope Project." Without being conscious of what we were doing, we visualized the movement of this change process as a cylinder. Every time we turn a kaleidoscope, a new picture with new possibilities is created. The movement of turning the cylinder stays the same, but the picture interacting with light changes every time. (See chapter 6 for a further exploration of how the cylinder-like organization can address the challenge of change.)

While we were implementing the Kaleidoscope Project in New York, I had started working for the Diocese of New Westminster of the Anglican Church in Vancouver, British Columbia. As the Ministry and Congregation Development Officer, I was charged with the ministry of helping local churches to grow and change. With the help of a group of committed lay and ordained leaders in the diocese, I implemented a second Kaleidoscope Project, using a similar format. In three years, we had made three "turns" of the Kaleidoscope Project in Vancouver and two more turns in New York. With the learning we gained from the feedback of congregation teams that had applied the model, we again modified the Process for Planned Change. In 1999, the Oklahoma Conference of the United Methodist Church invited me to implement three turns of the Kaleidoscope Project over a period of two years. The goal was not only to enable at least thirty congregations to implement change constructively using this model, but also to leave behind a local conference Kaleidoscope team to continue the work. The Kaleidoscope Process used in the Oklahoma conference was the most effective model we had taught to date. At the writing of this book, I am working out the details to implement one more turn for the Diocese of New York and three turns for the Baltimore-Washington Annual Conference of the United

Methodist Church. For the Baltimore-Washington Conference, we are calling this project the Human Mosaic Project.

This book is the first presentation of this material in written form. It consists of the learning we gained from working with more than seventy-five congregations through the Kaleidoscope Projects in New York, Vancouver, and Oklahoma. Chapters 1 and 2 describe why our churches are not able to respond constructively to the challenge of diversity today. Chapters 3 to 6 put forth the theories and theology supporting this change process. Chapters 7 to 8 give an overview of the Process of Planned Change. Chapter 9 functions like a workbook, taking a team of people from a church community through the Process for Planned Change step-by-step. The process utilizes the skills, theories, tools, and theology presented in my three previous books. Instead of repeating what I have written before, I have included reading assignments from those books. In that sense, chapter 9 can serve as a study guide for *The Wolf Shall Dwell with the Lamb, The Bush Was Blazing But Not Consumed*, and *Inclusion*.

The optimal way to use this book is to study it with a group of leaders from your church or ministry group. The first step is for you to covenant with others from your church for the time necessary to study together, explore together, pray together, and work through this process, trusting in God through the Holy Spirit to inspire and nurture you as you go. You can also study this book with leadership teams from other congregations. Regional denominational leaders may gather teams from three or four congregations to covenant for a time to come together and study and move through the change process presented in this book. There will be exercises and activities that you might want to facilitate for your team as well as for a larger group of people from the congregations involved.

The end result of working through the Process for Planned Change initially is the creation of an action plan for change with full accountability that your team will take back to your churches and implement. A faithful implementation of the plan will facilitate change. For some of you, the change for this first time might be a major transformation with profound change. For some of you, the change for this first time might be a project on a smaller scale; nevertheless, it is change in the faithful direction. Once you have learned this process you can implement it again and again. Each time you go through it, you enable the community to change a little more, and maybe by the third or even fourth time, the community will be ready for a more profound transformation.

The Process for Planned Change described in this book is not just something that you read as an intellectual exercise. To understand how this process actually works, you must apply it. In this book, I attempt to narrow the distance between discussing how to change and actually changing as we do the work. Do not just read about the theology of change, but live this theology so that you can become the catalyst for transformation. This process is an invitation to embody the gospel that gives us the courage to change, which in turn empowers us to invite others to enter this process by embodying the gospel in their community. Live Christ's life in your action. Don't just go to worship; live the worship in everything that you do. Don't just partake of the communion; be the body of Christ in every action that you take. Don't just observe the baptism; live the death and resurrection in your work, in your planning. Move through the planning process with Christ at the center, driving you forward to do justice and act with compassion. Don't just read the words, but be the Word. Let the Word become flesh and dwell among and in and through you, full of grace and truth.

CHAPTER 1

The Challenge of Diversity
So Complex, So Deep, So Wide, So Fast

I am writing this book on a two-year-old computer. In the computer world, this instrument into which I transfer my thoughts and knowledge is already a dinosaur. But I still cannot let go of the fact that when I bought this computer, it was the latest model with state-of-the-art software. I remember the happy days when I was writing my last book using this computer—it was faster than all the computers I had used before. I could almost write at the speed of my thoughts. But those happy days did not last. When a new version of the software that I had been using came out a year later, I enthusiastically upgraded my software, expecting it to work even faster and better. To my surprise, my computer became slow and sluggish. What used to take a fraction of a second was now taking seconds and sometimes even minutes. I called the computer manufacturer and inquired about how to fix this problem. After I gave the model number of my computer to the technical support person, I thought I heard him chuckle. Then he told me, "You've got an old computer. That's why." He proceeded to explain that the new software I loaded was designed for newer computers, which were at least ten times faster and had at least twenty times more memory. He added at the end of his explanation, "You need a new computer with more memory if you want to use the new software."

How could something that was so new become so old in such a short time? How could something that was once considered so big and fast become so small and slow in a year? How could something that was the top of the line become worthless so fast? My experience with my computer is only one indication of the depth and rate of change that has been happening all around us in the last twenty years. In the business world, this fast pace of change is an accepted fact of life. I was scanning the business books section of a local bookstore trying to get a sense of what the current business literature had to offer on the subject of organizational change. Titles dealing with change, such as *Change Is the Rule, The Dance of Change, The End of Change, Harvard Business Review on Change, Managing Transitions,* and *Discontinuous Change,* readily popped into my vision. There were also books on being able to move fast in order to compete, such as *It's Not the Big that Eat the Small...It's the Fast that Eat the Slow,* and *Business @ the Speed of Thought.* Business organizations are part of the world of rapid change. If change is the game, then businesses that want to compete must play that game. People working in the business world are forced to adjust to change every year, or even every month or every week, depending on what the "fashion for success" of the day is. If one does not adjust to the change fast enough, one might become the next victim that a company lets go during its next downsizing. There is even a book on dealing with what its author called "change fatigue." Total quality management, reengineering, restructuring and change-ready organizations are just a few of the terms used to denote these kinds of rapid changes required by the business world.

The racial diversity of the United States has also been undergoing a similar high-speed change. A couple of articles from *USA Today* in March 2001 summarized the result of the 2000 Census, which, according to the headline of one of the articles, highlights "racial diversity."

> About 2.4 percent, or 6.8 million of the country's 281 million people, checked off more than one race. Some chose combinations such as "white" and "black," and "white" and "Asian." Meanwhile the Hispanic population skyrocketed by about 58 percent over the last decade, up from 22.5 million in 1990 to 35.3 million in 2000. The number of non-Hispanic blacks meanwhile may have increased to as much as 21 percent from a decade ago, to 35.4 million...The non-Hispanic Asian population surged as much as 74 percent, to 11.6 million. The population of American Indians and [Hawaiian] Natives who were not Hispanic nearly doubled, up as much as 92 percent, to 3.4 million. The growth rate for non-Hispanic whites, meanwhile, lagged behind, up no more than 5.3 percent, to 198.2 million.

This means for every 100 people you meet, only 75 people could be non-Hispanic whites, 12 might identify themselves as non-Hispanic black, 12 or 13 might consider themselves Hispanics, 4 could be non-Hispanic Asians, 2 or 3 could be of mixed racial identity and 1 could be Native American or a Hawaiian Native. Another article in *USA Today,* on March 15, 2000, put it this way:

> There is nearly a 1 in 2 chance that two people selected at random in [the USA] are racially or ethnically different. USA TODAY used 2000 Census numbers released in this week to calculate the nation's diversity. The [diversity] index for 2000 is 49, up 23 percent from 40 in 1990. The index means there is a 49 percent chance two people are different...Much of the increase

in diversity is attributed to the rise in the number of Hispanics nationwide and even more dramatic increases in parts of the country that were not very diverse 10 years ago…In Kansas, for example, the Diversity Index rose from 21 in 1990 to 31 in 2000, although it was much higher in some parts of the state. In Finney County in southwestern Kansas, the index went from 26 to 59. Even in an already diverse state such as Texas, the index went from 55 to 62. And in a state with little diversity, such as Iowa, it went from 8 to 14. "It's not just a jump nationally," says Robert Lang, an urban expert at the Fannie Mae Foundation, who is analyzing census data for USA TODAY. "This translates to a good deal more local diversity as well."

The diversity challenge that we are experiencing is more complex, visible, and widespread than ever before. It is more complex because people are insisting on defining themselves with more specifics and often in multiple categories. For the first time, in the latest census survey, people could select more than one category, and many did. In the 2000 census, Americans had 63 racial categories to identify with, up from only five categories in 1990. Also, "Hispanic" is considered an ethnicity, not a race; people of Hispanic ethnicity can be of any race.

With the advance of technological innovation, this complex diversity has been spreading widely across the nation at a much faster pace than in the early and middle part of the last century. For example, improvement and accessibility in our travel technologies—faster trains and planes—have enabled people in the world to travel longer distance in less and less time. This ability to move quickly and at greater distances not only has supported the rapid increase in immigration, it also has spread the diversity of our population beyond our urban centers into communities all across the nation. Many of our communities are made up of strangers moving in for the opportunities that the community presents. When the opportunities cease, they move away in search of new chances elsewhere. It is becoming harder and harder to find neighborhoods where people have lived for generations and have known and supported each other over the years.[1] For example, in 1971, my family immigrated to the United States and settled in Chinatown, New York City, a typical urban center where new immigrants have converged for centuries. While my mother still lives in New York City, all her children are spread across the continent pursuing the opportunities that were presented to them. Of my four siblings, one is an electrical engineer who moved his family from New York City to New Jersey and then to the Bay area of California, where he lives now. Another brother is an artist who moved from New York to Baltimore, then to St. Louis, and finally settled in Portland, Oregon, three years ago. I moved from New York City to Corning, a small town in Central New York State for my first job, then to Cambridge for graduate school, then to Los Angeles, and then to Vancouver, B.C., and finally moved back to Southern California last year. Only my sister still lives near my mother in Westchester, a suburb of New York City. Diversity is no longer an urban phenomenon; it has been spreading rapidly to many rural areas, suburban towns, and smaller cities.

Adding to this complex and widespread diversity is the unwillingness of people who are not part of the power-holders of society to keep silent and just survive. The various minority groups who make up this complex diversity are demanding to be accepted, understood, and appreciated for who they are. The civil rights movement starting in the 1960s was the first to challenge the historically dominant group's control and assumptions. The women's movement in the '70s and '80s drastically changed the way we see the roles of women in the

---

[1]See Leith Anderson, *Dying for Change* (Minneapolis: Bethany House Publishers, 1990), pp.26–41. Anderson named ten predictable categories of changes in the U.S.: mobility, coloring, graying, women, pluralism, shifts in segmentation, short-term commitments, decline in the work ethic, conservatism, and cocooning. All these are somehow related to technology and mobility.

church and society. The gay and lesbian liberation movements in the last twenty years have challenged the core values and assumptions about sexuality, relationship, and intimacy, in both the church and society.

Again, innovation in media technologies has played a major part in these movements. Media technologies have enabled these previously silenced voices to be heard on a much wider scale. When these alternate voices are heard and accepted by more and more people, then what used to be an absolute and core principle to the historically dominant group has instead become just one of many choices. What used to be the only way to do something is now only one of many ways. The same media technologies that enabled these voices to be heard continue to develop faster and faster (from the wealth of special-interest channels on cable and satellite TV to the proliferation of Web sites on the Internet), allowing us to access a mind-boggling array of choices on everything with which we come into contact. The media's presentation of these choices is often without any value judgment, however, making them all relative to each other. In this way, pluralism becomes an assumed reality.

The increasingly vocal and diverse population has moved the Christian church away from being the "sponsor of culture" in the United States. What used to be called "the Christmas holiday" is now called "winter vacation." What used to be called "Easter Break" is now called "Spring Break," and it no longer is always the same weekend as Easter (in fact, some states stagger their "Spring Break" with those of neighboring states, so that in a given year, only some regions will actually get Holy Week off). Going to church is just one among many alternative things to do on Sundays. Parents today have to decide whether to take their children to team-sport practice, ballet lessons, or church on Sundays. The Christian church is no longer perceived as the center of people's lives, nor even as the center of our society. A number of Christian writers have suggested that we are living in a "Post-Christian" era. "Confused and uncertain, the church today is more likely to be concerned about its own future than its influence; security and survival have priority over missional engagement with our postmodern culture. The church has been pushed to the margins of society—it is now marginalized."[2]

The increase in cultural diversity not only moves away from the center the assumption of our nation as Christian, thereby making this relative to other perspectives, it also challenges the deep-seated Eurocentric assumptions of the church at a deep and profound level. The Christian church has had a long history of European influence. Many North American churches have taken these European assumptions for granted as if they are what life should be—"normal." When members of the church were also the historically dominant group of our government, their Eurocentric Christian patterns also shaped the patterns and myths of the nation. In this post-Christian time, "the core traits that formed the culture of North America are in the process of radical transformation and disembedding. Not only are they being uprooted, these core values are now in competition with core traits that have arrived from all parts of the world as a multi-cultural society emerges on this continent. The particular culture that formed the inner life of Christian identity is also being challenged and uprooted precisely on account of the larger cultural shifts, the disembedding of Christian life from its former role of prime sponsor of the larger culture."[3]

The complex, widespread, vocal, and diverse population poses profound and unsettling challenges to the church that has been steeped in its Eurocentric core assumptions, patterns, and myths. With the assistance of technology, these deep and profound challenges are coming at the church at increasing frequency, like the colliding of deep and strong underwater currents, which cause the water on the surface of the river of

---

[2]Alan Roxburgh, *Crossing the Bridge—Church Leadership in a Time of Change* (Costa Mesa, Calif. : Percept Group, Inc., 2000), p. 24.
[3]Ibid., p. 100.

society to move in unexpected directions with extraordinary force and speed. "We no longer experience the river of time as a slow, peaceful stream with quiet eddies and calm pools where we have ample opportunity to regain our equilibrium or to recoup our energies. We are instead white-water rafting through the rapids of social, technological, and demographic change. We are shooting down a foaming river filled with unexpected whirlpools and turbulent, rock-strewn…channels."[4]

Many churches still stubbornly hold on to the old paradigm that assumes the church is still the "sponsor of culture." They are puzzled, lost, and confused. Like me, still writing on this dinosaur of a computer, and not willing to spend the energy and resources to buy and learn the latest technology, many of our churches are not willing to face the reality of this rapidly changing society. Instead of learning new ways to be faithful in this new environment, they hold on to behaviors, structures, assumptions, rules, and myths of the past that are no longer relevant, effective, or applicable. In the next chapter, we will examine further why some of the churches' responses to the challenge of diversity are ineffective. Then we will explore, in subsequent chapters, what is a faithful response to this challenge and how we can move our churches toward it, both theologically and practically.

---

[4]Thomas R. Hawkins, *The Learning Congregation—A New Vision of Leadership* (Louisville: Westminster John Knox Press, 1997), p. 3.

CHAPTER 2

The Churches' Response to the Challenge of Diversity

Too Scared, Too Shallow, Too Much, Too Slow

Imagine what life is like during the week for adults sitting in church on Sunday morning. What might be on their minds, living in what seems to be a permanent whitewater society?

"They just changed the policy and structure of the company again. What used to be right last week is wrong this week! Am I going to be able to adjust to the new changes in my work and survive the next downsizing?"

"What *are* my kids learning from the Internet these days? I don't even know what they are talking about most of the time."

"Another shooting happened in a school this week. I shouldn't have to worry about whether my kids are going to get shot when they go to school!"

"The stock market went down again for the fifth time this month. I might lose a lot of money if it doesn't go back up soon."

"I had to find a new way to get to church today because they're widening the road to carry all the extra traffic in the neighborhood because of that new development down the way. And it's bringing all those 'unfriendly' people into the neighborhood."

"I don't understand why people have to have so many labels for themselves in the Census 2000 data. Why do they have to be different and demand their rights? Why can't we just be Americans?"

By the time many people get to church, they are totally exhausted from the changes they have had to face every day in order to survive. When they see changes in church, they might react in the following ways:

"What? We're doing a bilingual liturgy today! Nobody told me that!"

"Whatever happened to the good old hymns that we used to sing? You call *this* music?!"

"Why can't people learn to behave properly in church? I do. Why can't they?"

Many church members instinctively want the church to be a place of refuge from the turbulent world out there. Church becomes a place where they want to hold on to some semblance of certainty in a world of uncertainty, relativism, and pluralism. Church becomes a place where they can hold on to their sense of control and power because out there, their power seems to be slipping away. Church becomes a place where they want to make sure that they know what is right or wrong. They hold on to the rules (both explicit and implicit ones) and say, "We've never done it that way before." They might want to fix their worship in time, recapturing the glory days of the past. They calcify their rules and regulations in their church, making "a golden calf" for themselves.[1] They dance around it, thinking

---

[1]For a more in-depth discussion of the "Golden Calf Syndrome," see chapter 5 of Eric H. F. Law, *The Bush Was Blazing But Not Consumed* (St. Louis: Chalice Press, 1996), pp. 26–35.

that they are doing something to address these changes around them, but they are in fact going around in circles, going nowhere fast.

Meanwhile, church attendance continues to decline, yet they reassure themselves that their church is a friendly, welcoming church. Why wouldn't anyone want to come and join their church, since everyone knows it is a great refuge from the turbulent change in the world? So they dance around their golden calf one more time. They are so scared that they just sit on a rock refusing to acknowledge the whitewater rapids rushing by them. They fool themselves into believing that they are safe on their rock, but all the time they are feeling a sense of loss and confusion from being left behind, isolated and cut off from the flow of the world.

Some churches realize that they have to do something to increase the membership of the church or else the church will face financial difficulty. If church members do not do this with some degree of self-reflection, they will simply employ techniques, skills, and methods of change that once worked in the world they knew. In that old paradigm, the church was the sponsor of culture; all they needed to do in order to respond to any challenge was to maintain and adjust what they already had. These methods only deal with surface behavior and do not address the deep and profound challenges that they are facing today. Authors who write about organizational change call this approach to change a technical, or incremental, change that does not require the members to examine their deep-seated assumptions, patterns, and myths; nor does it require them to recognize and adjust to the major paradigm shift that has occurred. They tend to think that if they keep doing what they have always done, only better, the situation will change. A typical response might be: "If we make sure everybody knows their parts better in the worship service, people will come and they'll like us and they'll stay."

Some churches blame the leadership for their predicament, especially their pastor. When a church recognizes signs of decline in its attendance, buildings, or budget, the most popular response is to change the clergy. They perform all kinds of studies to determine what kind of pastor they need. They even go through a whole process of setting goals that they want the new pastor to help them accomplish. They expect the new pastor to lead them out of their troubled waters. It all looks good on paper, but when the new pastor arrives and tries to implement some of the changes, invariably a group of vocal church members resist by saying, "That's not how we do things here."

Some churches would say, "Let's make it a policy that every member must be friendly to our newcomers from now on." When they try implementing that new rule, they discover that the newcomers are very uncomfortable when church members swarm around them like flies at a picnic, asking if they will come back. The neediness of such a church actually winds up driving the newcomers away. So attendance continues to decline. Meanwhile, they are really experiencing financial problems; they are spending more and more time during their meetings talking about the budget. Someone says, "What we need is a better stewardship campaign. Let's make everyone pledge to give a few percent more of his or her income. That's what the Bible says." But giving only goes up a little—and it still is not enough.

Someone suggests that what they need is better youth programs. So they find some money, get a grant, and hire a youth minister. But the youth program only attracts a small group. Someone else suggests that they need an outreach program to welcome all the diverse people living in the neighborhood. They then muster up their energy and resources and try that. The reason that this form of outreach fails is that it does not focus on serving the real needs of the people in the wider community, but rather on the self-preservation of the congregation. They want newcomers so that they can continue their way of life in their castle, away from the turbulence of change. As a result, they do not gain any new members, nor do they improve their financial picture. They jump into whatever is the latest "successful" program that they have read about or hear about and say, "Let's do that. If it worked for them over there, it should work for us."[2]

Churches that work very hard to change in shallow water without addressing the challenges found in the deep, rushing currents often find themselves exactly where they were in the beginning, but more exhausted and with fewer resources. Yes, it has taken some courage for them to jump into the white water. They are bobbing and dragging on the surface, trying every possible method to stay afloat, to not be washed away. They hold onto branches of the past—the old paradigm—in order to stay alive. Without addressing the deep cross-current underneath them, they will continue to exhaust their energy and resources by going nowhere. As one of the churches that I worked with discovered, "We are trying so hard to survive that we have forgotten how to be faithful in this changing world."

Many church communities recognize the deep and profound challenges that our diverse society poses for them. Some have even learned that changing on the surface by using old assumptions and patterns will not work. They may finally decide that they need a long-range plan that will help them renew their mission, guiding them through this difficult time. They spend an enormous amount of time collecting information—focus groups, surveys, demographic data, etc. Then they laboriously analyze the data. Next, they spend another large amount of time drafting and redrafting a mission or vision statement that describes for them the place they want to be in three or five years. Once the statement has been written, they must deal with all the people who resist the proposed change. They may suffer some setbacks, but they persevere.

Finally, they manage to get everyone to agree on the vision. They actually follow through with their action plan, and three

---

[2]Gilbert R. Rendle called this the "three Ps" of quick fixes—people, policy, and program. See Gilbert R. Rendle, *Leading Change in the Congregation* (Alban Institute Publication, 1989), pp. 35–36.

or five years later they accomplish their goals. They have in fact changed in a very profound way and have ultimately arrived at their new vision. Exhausted from the process, they swear that they will not do it again for a long time. Although they think they can rest awhile, they discover that the world around them has changed while they were working so hard on their own transformation. The changes they worked so hard for now seem obsolete and irrelevant. Like my two-year-old computer, it still feels new but is already a dinosaur.

I remember all the long-range planning programs that many regions of my denomination facilitated during the 1980s. Most of them were linear processes—that is, the change process takes the organization from where they are to where they want to be. As in a race, there is a finish line. As in a football game, we have to deal with the "enemy" who resists change along the way. This kind of approach to change worked well when the world was not changing so quickly. We had the luxury of doing long-range planning, of getting there and resting for a while before the next wave of change came our way. Denominational leaders had successfully facilitated this kind of change in local churches, especially during times of transition, such as the time between the departure of the old pastor and the arrival of the new. But this kind of process is cumbersome and often meets with much resistance, resulting in too much intensive work for a long period of time. Even if the process is successful, the resulting change may come too slowly and be too costly to meet the challenge of rapid changes in the world around us.

We are living in a permanent whitewater society. Some of us may be too scared to deal with this rapid and profound challenge. So we avoid getting too close to the rapids, thereby cutting ourselves off from the flow of things. Some of us may be willing to work on facing the situation, but we only use methods that are too shallow to address the deep challenges of diversity that we are facing. As a result, our initiatives and hard work only leave us exhausted and with few results. Some of us may be willing to face the challenges by examining our assumptions and by engaging ourselves in a deeper transformation. But the process that we use may sap our energy and resources—and the resulting change, profound as it may be, might come too slowly to meet the fast pace of change all around us.

CHAPTER 3

Called to Be in the World and Not of the World

Toward a Faithful Response to Diversity

*"I am not asking you to take them out of the world, but I ask
you to protect them from the evil one. They do not belong to the
world, just as I do not belong to the world. Sanctify them in the
truth; your word is truth. As you have sent me into the world, so
I have sent them into the world. And for their sakes I sanctify
myself, so that they also may be sanctified in truth."*

(JOHN 17:15–19)

What then are the effective and faithful responses to the
challenge of diversity? We learned from the last chapter that
staying within our safe zone—holding on to our old
paradigm—will not work. On the other hand, if we move out
of our safe zone and step into today's permanent whitewater
society full of challenges that pull, push, and tug at our core

values, assumptions, and patterns, we might lose ourselves, our identities, and even our faith. We might complain, "When the world is changing so fast and everything becomes so relative, we don't know what is right or wrong anymore." This uncertainty is unbearable, especially because the church was the sponsor of culture for so long. We might become afraid and retreat back to our safe zones, holding on to the old paradigm even tighter. We might justify that by saying, "When everything is relative, we must hold on to our faith, because our faith is the only thing that stays constant." We might even quote the scriptural passage in which Jesus said that we do not belong to the world as he did not belong to the world. Therefore, we claim that we must stand firm and hold on to what we have and refuse to acknowledge the changes that are happening all around us. There seems to be no grace margin between our safe zones and fear zones when it comes to dealing with the complex challenges of diversity. How can we help our churches to stretch and find the grace margin[1] where the word of God is spoken and lived and within which we may find the courage to address these challenges in truth?

As disciples of Christ, we do not belong to the world as Jesus did not belong to the world (Jn. 17:16). However, we cannot be so afraid of the world that we isolate ourselves from it and therefore are not even in it to do God's will. Jesus came into the world to live among us as a common human being, but he was not of the world because he insisted on challenging the world with the truth—the truth of God's justice and compassion. We are called by Christ to do the same, to challenge the world by first entering into it. "As you have sent me into the world, so I have sent them into the world" (Jn. 17:17). To live as faithful people, we must not avoid the world, but find the courage to enter it, knowing God will protect us.

---

[1]For a full exposition of the concept of "grace margin," see chapter 4 of Eric H. F. Law, *Inclusion—Making Room for Grace* (St. Louis: Chalice Press, 2000), pp. 39–48.

We must not deny people's need for security and stability. But we must not give in to the temptation to provide stability through holding on to external things, rules and rituals, making them absolute and unchanging—making them into idols. These things are not our faith. They are but expressions of our faith from our unique context at one point in past time. We must not give in to our fear of the change around us by holding on to our power and control in the governance of our church. Power and control are temporary means to gain a sense of stability, but they do not last and they are certainly not of our faith.

> Do not love the world or the things in the world...And the world and its desire are passing away, but those who do the will of God live forever. (1 John 2:15, 17)

When we focus on doing the will of God, we will have the courage to step out of our safe zone. As faithful Christians, our security comes from knowing that God will be with us no matter what happens. Our safety comes from knowing that Christ will be close to our hearts when we take that leap of faith and step outside our safe boundary. With this assurance, we are not scared of the world, and can bravely enter it to do the will of God.

Once we dive into the fast-paced, ever-changing, pluralistic world, what do we do? With all the different forces coming at us from different directions—pushing, coming over us from above and drawing us out from under—how do we move in this world without losing ourselves, our identities, or our faithfulness? How can we stop ourselves from becoming so frightened that we retreat to the comfort of our safe zone?

In the business world, change is not a bad word. Businesses change because the world is changing, and their customers are changing, whether in terms of demographics, needs, or wants. And their competitors are changing as well. Whoever can change the fastest will be the one to make more money. If you don't change fast enough, you will not survive. The raison d'être of change in the business world boils down to this phrase: survival and profit. Even though the purpose of the church is not to make a profit, the need to survive in this turbulent time has pushed many churches into employing the business world's techniques and methods of adapting to change. With a few exceptions, these change processes are often linear and utilize imageries from war and competitive sports. They assume that the organization knows what it wants to change and then sets out to impose that change. There is endless talk about fighting the resistance and pushing toward accomplishing their stated goals.

I was having a conversation with a young and energetic pastor who had tried to implement change in his church. In order to prepare for this, he studied all the literature on techniques and models for change. He said, "So much of the literature talks about the people who resist change as if they were the enemy, the evil ones to be fought against and overcome. Some even talk about giving up on them and starting over somewhere else. I can't do that. They are members of the body of Christ, too. They've been members of the church for a long time. I found those models not to be very helpful at all." This is the problem with many of the change processes that were borrowed from the business community. How do you wage a war on your brothers and sisters who have been in the church for so many years? It is perfectly understandable why they are afraid and therefore why they resist any change. Surely we do not have to view them as adversaries. If we demonize those who do not want to change, treating them as the enemy that we have to fight against, we have become part "of the world."

As Christians, we do not change simply because we want to survive, like most organizations of the world do. We do not change because it is the latest fashion for success. We must not fall into the temptation to become part "of the world" once we enter it. We must discover the reason for change that is not "of the world" but of God.

> Do not be conformed to this world, but be transformed
> by the renewing of your minds, so that you may discern
> what is the will of God. (Romans 12:2)

We change because we are *doing* God's will in the world. We change in order to present Christ anew to a world that has changed and is still changing. We change because we are willing to die to our old self and rise again in the new life of Christ. We change because we encounter God in our hearts and our actions, and in that encounter, we are transformed. In being transformed, we reconnect with the body of Christ and use the presence of the Word to transform the world. We change because we have renewed our minds so that we may discern and do the will of God.

We are called to live in the tension between living "in the world" and not being "of the world." Somewhere in between having the courage to dive into the whitewater rapids of this changing world and yet not becoming the whitewater itself is where we need to find the grace margin to address the challenge of change and diversity. We cannot avoid being in the world, for we have been sent into the world. And we will always face the danger of becoming "of the world," and in so doing, losing our faith. In order to live in this grace margin, we must focus our minds and hearts on what is "of God" and "of the Spirit."

> Now we have received not the spirit of the world, but
> the Spirit that is from God, so that we may understand
> the gifts bestowed on us by God. (1 Corinthians 2:12)

What is it like living in this creative tension of being in the world and yet not being of the world? Hawkins, who gave us the image of the permanent whitewater society, suggested four rules he learned from a whitewater rafting instructor that apply to ministry in this world.

1. Rest in the calm spots, because there are always more rapids ahead.

2. When heading for a rock, lean into the rock rather than away from it.
3. Never stop paddling.
4. Let go of everything but your life jacket if you fall into the water.[2]

Let us explore each one of these techniques in more detail.

1. Rest in the calm spots, because there are always more rapids ahead.

These calm spots are becoming rarer to find. We might need to intentionally find the time and space in our busy lives to reflect on our experiences—to learn from our mistakes and to affirm the positive and effective things that we have done so that we can better anticipate the rapids ahead. This is a time to celebrate our accomplishments and give thanks to God for leading us through the turbulence. But we need to be mindful not to stay too long, or we might be in danger of being left behind, isolated once again from the world and retreating to our safe zone. Consider reading and working through this book as one of those moments of calm when we find time and space to reflect on ourselves, our community, and the way our faith can interface with the world. It is only then that we can discern what is God's will for us. We reconnect with Christ's courage to face his Passion. We open our hearts to receive the Spirit of God to guide us, to sustain us through the journey. We renew our covenant with each other and with God—our lifejackets before we reenter the rapids.

2. When heading for a rock, lean into the rock rather than away from it.

We must not avoid facing problems and dangers while we are in the world. Most organizations' survival instincts cause them to steer away from the rock to avoid the danger. As

---

[2]Thomas R. Hawkins, *The Learning Congregation—A New Vision of Leadership* (Louisville: Westminster John Knox Press, 1997), pp. 19–20.

Christians, we do not change because we need to survive. Contrary to our survival instinct, Christians are called to die so that new life can emerge. Hawkins called this "counterintuitive."[3] At the heart of our Christian faith is the death and resurrection of Christ. That is the ultimate Christian challenge for change. To discern God's will means that we are not to avoid the difficult issues presented by the challenge of diversity, but we are to lean into it. We are to look at it, see the danger of it, and differentiate between the world's way of dealing with it and God's will for us. We must learn to face our problems and our perceived enemy but refuse to use the ways of the world to deal with them—the ways of domination, control, legalistic maneuvers, power plays, and threats. If we are faithful, we must work through the difficult spots with love and charity, with one hand holding on to justice and the other to compassion. We must let go of the ways of the world and reconnect with the way of God. In the next chapter, we will explore in depth how "leaning into the rock" works by using an analytical tool called the "Iceberg Analogy of Culture."

3. Never stop paddling.

When we paddle in the rapids, we are participating and becoming part of the forces that make up the experience, as opposed to simply flowing along with the current or avoiding it altogether. Each time we put the paddle in the water and exert our force and energy, we are interacting with the current. It is the interaction between the force we apply to the paddle and the force and direction of the current that determines the raft's new movements. Even though paddling is a repeated movement, the circumstances are different every time we apply our force to the paddle, because the current has changed, and we learn something new. When we are paddling, we do not become part of the white water but are interacting with it,

---

[3]Ibid., p. 19.

sometimes working against it when we see injustice, sometimes flowing with it when we see God's justice and compassion already at work. In order to stay faithful and yet still challenge the fast-changing, turbulent world, we must learn to practice paddling—the cyclical skills and processes that we can use again and again by interacting, redirecting, resisting, and maximizing the force of the current. Remember that we do not do this alone. There are other committed people who are also learning and who are also paddling with us (see chapter 7). More importantly, we come together to learn to paddle with Christ through this turbulent world. It is my hope that through this book, readers will learn how to paddle with Christ. We will explore these cyclical transforming processes in chapter 6.

4. Let go of everything but your life jacket if you fall into the water.

As Christians, we must be change-ready in order to do ministry in a changing world. However, we do not change for change's sake. We are not promoting a gospel of change, but the gospel of Jesus Christ. We do not jump in the water without holding on to the gospel, the heart of our faith. Sometimes the gospel calls us to let go of everything that is supposed to keep us safe, including our boat and our paddles, knowing that the good news of Jesus Christ is still close to our hearts, giving us courage, power, and the spirit to go on. For as Christians, our safety comes not from holding onto external things, rules or rituals, but rather our dynamic relationship with God through Christ. Jesus faced the cross with nothing but his relationship with God. We must have the courage to do the same, knowing that there will be resurrection on the other side. When we know how to hold on to this dynamic relationship with God through Christ, we are then empowered to make changes in our lives and our communities according to God's will, not ours.

We keep this dynamic relationship with God alive through the liturgies of our lives and work. I do not mean just the liturgy that we participate in on Sunday. Everything we do should be a liturgy in which we keep our relationship with God through Christ in front of us. At every step of our planned-change process, we ask not for what we want, but for what God wants us to do and change.

By giving thanks, remembering, and reenacting the death and resurrection of our Lord Jesus Christ in our planning and working, we allow God to change our hearts of fear into hearts of flesh, of compassion, of love, and of passion for justice and peace. We become doers of God's word, not just hearers (Jas. 1:22). In the liturgy of our lives and work, we become Christ's body—Christ's eyes, ears, hands, and feet. Together, we act with compassion to effect change for justice.

CHAPTER 4

Digging Down Deep to
Facilitate Profound Change

After four months of exploration and reflection on why they were not able to grow, members of a shrinking, aging congregation arrived at the following action plan. They took out the last two pews in the back of the church and set up a quiet play area for children. When newcomers with young children came to church, they could leave their children right there and worship in the church, knowing their children would be near them and safe. Their goal was *to become a church that welcomed families with children,* and by doing that, they hoped to increase their membership by 15 percent in six months. Within a month, nineteen new children and their parents were coming to church consistently. They had exceeded their modest goal in a fraction of the time set forth in their action plan. Word of their success traveled quickly to other parts of the denomination.

A group of leaders in another church heard about this success story and decided that they would implement the same idea. They said, "We are in the exact same situation that this church was in—an aging congregation, unable to attract younger newcomers with children. If this idea works for them, then it should work for us. It's simple enough to do." When they removed the last two pews, the whole congregation was up in arms about it. People complained that they were not consulted on this change. They grumbled, "Without those last two pews, the church just isn't the same. And by the way, what happened to the little brass memorial plates on the sides of these pews?" Of course, when they did have children in the play area, they complained about the noise and the bad behavior of the children. Within a month, that church had restored everything to the way it was previously. They did not gain any new young families with children.

Why do some of these techniques work well in some places and not in others? The reason why the idea worked for the first congregation was that there was a change in the fundamental perception of the church members about themselves and the community around them. In four months spent reflecting on their issues, they had moved the congregation from operating out of a maintenance model to a missionary model of church.[1] The external change was accompanied by an internal transformation. This kind of internal change has been called many different names by many writers on organizational change: transformational change, adaptive change, reorientation, recreation, discontinuous change, changing the organizational culture, paradigm shift, deep change, and profound change. They all point to a deeper internal change that accompanies the external change of behavior, structure, and system.

Peter Senge et al., in *The Dance of Change*, explained this kind of change this way: Profound change is "organizational

---

[1]For a detailed comparison of maintenance and missionary models, see Claude E. Payne and Hamilton Beazley, *Reclaiming the Great Commission* (San Francisco: Jossey-Bass, 2000), pp. 48–49.

change that combines inner shifts in people's values, aspirations, and behaviors with 'outer' shifts in processes, strategies, practices, and systems. The word 'profound' stems from the Latin *fundus*, a base or foundation. It means, literally, 'moving toward the fundamental.' In profound change there is learning. The organization doesn't just do something new; it builds its capacity for doing things in a new way—indeed, it builds capacity for ongoing change. This emphasis on inner and outer changes gets to the heart of the issues…It is not enough to change strategies, structures, and systems, unless the thinking that produced these strategies, structures, and systems also changes."[2]

Alan Roxburgh in his book *Crossing the Bridge* said that this kind of transition is not a linear one, through which we try to move our church community from one set of behaviors and structures to another. "It is about reconnecting with the core story and tradition so that they are freed from the old frameworks. When this happens, there is freedom to recognize the values and frameworks that must be released so that our systems can move toward the reinventing of a missional future."[3]

In order to accomplish this profound change, the first step is to find a way to discover the old frameworks, assumptions, and patterns that are no longer appropriate or relevant in responding to the challenges and changes around us. Since these frameworks, assumptions, and patterns have developed over a long period of time, most church members may have become largely unconscious of their development. The crucial step to our change model is to reveal these mostly unconscious, unspoken assumptions. Once we can see and articulate them, we can then entertain the possibility of changing them.

Church leaders have come to me time and time again and reported that the moment they realized that their church could change was when the church members could finally discuss the "unspeakable." To help readers understand what this step

---

[2]Peter Senge et al., *The Dance of Change* (New York: Doublday, 1999), p. 15.
[3]Alan Roxburgh, *Crossing the Bridge—Church Leadership in a Time of Change* (Costa Mesa, Calif.: Percept Group, Inc., 2000), p. 61.

involves, I will again utilize the "iceberg analogy."[4] This is an image I used in my first book, *The Wolf Shall Dwell with the Lamb*, to help people understand intercultural conflicts. The following is an expanded description of this analogy, applying it to organization change.

An iceberg has a small piece above the water that we can easily see, and a much larger irregular piece submerged under the water that we cannot see, nor do we know it is even there. Throughout history, the submerged parts of icebergs have been responsible for many shipwrecks precisely because they could not be seen. The part above the water represents the external culture and the part under the water represents the internal cultural of an organization. Profound change happens not with the external culture of the organization; it must occur from a transformation of the internal culture. Let us apply this analogy to our church organization, starting with the external culture of the church.

Figure 4.1
Iceberg Analogy of Organization Culture

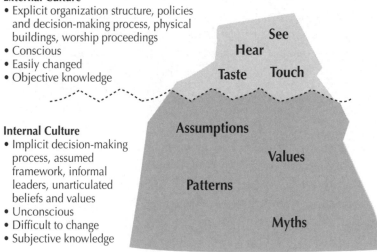

External Culture
- Explicit organization structure, policies and decision-making process, physical buildings, worship proceedings
- Conscious
- Easily changed
- Objective knowledge

See
Hear
Taste   Touch

Internal Culture
- Implicit decision-making process, assumed framework, informal leaders, unarticulated beliefs and values
- Unconscious
- Difficult to change
- Subjective knowledge

Assumptions
Values
Patterns
Myths

---

[4]Eric H. F. Law, *The Wolf Shall Dwell with the Lamb* (St. Louis: Chalice Press, 1993), pp. 4–10.

In the organizational culture of the church, the part above the water—the external culture—includes the appearance of the physical buildings of the church, our worship proceedings, our music, our doctrine, our explicit organizational structure and decision-making process, our stated mission, and so on. These are the things that we can see, hear, taste, and touch. We are conscious of their existence. We can readily articulate why they are there. A purely external cultural element of an organization is very easily changed to adapt to something new. Usually these are changes that do not require changing or shifting of the core assumptions, frameworks, and patterns of the organization. In other words, the kinds of changes at this level are not profound changes.

For example, the old water fountain located by the bathroom of a church broke down. The building and grounds committee met and decided to replace the fountain with a freestanding water dispenser from a distilled water company that would deliver water every week. In the meeting, committee members arrived at this decision for the following reasons:

1. The tap water coming out of the fountain was full of minerals and did not taste very good.
2. The reason the fountain broke down was because of the mineral build-up from the unfiltered water.
3. A check of the budget indicated they could afford the new water dispenser with the ongoing cost of water delivery and the cost of paper cups.

They voted on it and added the item into the budget permanently. In a week, the dispenser was in place and everyone appreciated it. This was purely an external cultural change, and the reasons behind the decision were very clear. They were dealing with something they could see and taste and touch, the objective was clear, and the group consciously made the decision and the change.

Many authors of change models refer to this purely external cultural change as technical change, surface change, or incremental change. It is technical, because it requires only the changing of the physical arrangement of things. It is only changing things on the surface, because it does not require any change of the deeper core assumptions of the church. It is incremental because the added budget item constitutes a small addition to the overall structure of the budget, and it does not require a shift in paradigm in people's perception of the church. This change does not challenge the deeply held assumptions, frameworks, patterns, and myths of the community.

If every change in church were purely a change at the external cultural level, we would not need this book to teach us how to change. All the quick fixes described in chapter 2— people, programs and policy—would work beautifully. But, as most of us who have attempted to implement change in the church know, change often involves more than just changing the physical environment or people's behavior. For example, if the water fountain was donated by a very prominent member of the church, the change described above might not be as simple. Since there is a myth deep in the organizational iceberg attached to this object, replacing it would require more than just an explicit rational discussion. More often than not, when we move something that seems like a purely external cultural element, we encounter major inertia. It feels as if we are dragging a lot of things that we cannot even name.

I was invited to consult with a church that was struggling with what they called the "kitchen" problem. The complaint initially came from the people who worshipped at the 9 a.m. English-speaking service.

"The Korean congregation at 11 o'clock comes into the kitchen way too early," they griped. "We almost never get to use the kitchen to prepare for our coffee hour."

I asked them, "What have you done to address this problem?"

They said they put up a schedule on the kitchen wall stating very clearly that from 8:30 to 10:30 a.m. the kitchen is to be used by the English-speaking congregation only, and from

10:30 a.m. to 1 p.m., the kitchen is to be used by the Korean congregation. They seemed to be addressing this problem purely from an external cultural level at this point. I asked them if the schedule worked to solve their problem.

"It kind of worked for a while, but now we are hearing complaints about who stinks up the kitchen with what smell."

As I had suspected, the problem had transformed itself into something else. So I asked them what they did this time to address the new complaint.

"We put up another sign and we bought a large can of odor neutralizer. The sign says, 'SPRAY BEFORE YOU GO.'"

"Did that work?" I asked.

"Not really. Now we are hearing complaints about the Korean children running around the parish hall and the kitchen, and making too much noise."

When we address a seemingly external problem by using an external solution but the problem does not go away, then we are dealing with more than just the external culture. We must look at the internal culture, the part of the organization's iceberg that is below the water. The real issue from the above example was that in the submerged part, two very different icebergs were bumping against each other. The presence of the growing Korean congregation posed a major challenge to the assumed framework, pattern, and myths of the English-speaking congregation. The complaints about the kitchen were just the surface expression of the apprehension of this unconscious challenge.

Let me offer another example. In the 1960s, we observed the people in the South being segregated—that is, people of difference races were not mixing. If we simply treated that as an external cultural issue, an external cultural solution would be to physically mix people of different races together. The most well-known approach of this kind was "busing." We bused people of different races to one place and forced them to mix together in one classroom. But that did not solve our problem of segregation. Instead, the people who were forced together did not get along. There were tensions, conflicts, and even physical violence. But we still thought that was only an external cultural problem. So we implemented another external solution. When people fought, we just needed to stop them. So we sent in law enforcement to stop them from fighting. This did not solve the problem; it only complicated it some more. The real issue was that the cultural icebergs of the different racial groups were colliding under the water. Both groups challenged each other's assumptions, patterns, myths, and cultural frameworks at the unconscious level. If we were to move both groups toward constructive change, we had to address the issue from that deeper level. Profound change has to come from exploring the internal part of our cultural icebergs.

The internal culture is the larger irregular part below the water level of our cultural iceberg. These are beliefs and values that we have implicitly learned. They are below our consciousness and therefore very difficult to change. They are patterns in our lives that we have accepted as normal. They consist of myths—stories that we learned when we were young, like fairy tales, or events and stories from past generations that have, over time, sunk to the bottom of our cultural iceberg.

Even though these myths and patterns are outside our consciousness, they still condition the way we perceive and react to the world around us. They are subjective knowledge. They are there, but we cannot explain it. For example, a child asks, "Why do we do it this way?" Many of us might find ourselves saying something like, "Because I said so," or simply "Because!" This is not something objective that we teach our children. We are teaching them something subjective, a pattern with no explanation, an unspoken value or belief that is unconscious.

Let me illustrate the connection between the external and internal culture by using another example from education. A teacher says to a class, "Your class participation counts a lot for your final grade." This is the external part of what is taught; we can hear the teacher say it, we are conscious of this saying, and perhaps we even believe that it is objective. But let us examine what this statement might teach us implicitly in our internal culture in the United States.

When we say "class participation," we usually mean speaking on behalf of oneself. This is not a universal concept. In Hong Kong, where I grew up, we were given a grade for class participation also. However, our class participation was measured by how well we did not stand out from the group with which we were working. This was a very different concept of participation, shaping a very different internal cultural iceberg for the students in Hong Kong.

Let us come back to the internal cultural iceberg of the United States, where participation means speaking on behalf of oneself. If a class is one hour long and has thirty students, equal participation of everyone would mean each student has two minutes to participate. But that rarely happens, because the teacher usually speaks for about forty-five minutes in most of the classes I have attended. If the teacher speaks for forty-five minutes, we only have fifteen minutes left for thirty students to participate. In the United States, we say out loud on the external cultural level that all people are equal. So if everyone is equal, each student can only have thirty seconds to participate. But that is physically impossible, because if a student talks and the teacher responds, that exchange usually takes up two minutes, so that with the remaining fifteen minutes, only seven or eight students out of thirty can really participate. What might this be teaching our students implicitly and unconsciously?

When I described the above scenario in a workshop and posited the same question, participants would eventually arrive at the conclusion that we are teaching our students "competition for time." Not only are we teaching them competition, we are teaching them a concept of time. Time is a commodity: if they are to do well in this class, they have to claim their share of time. They have learned that time is worth a lot to their grade. Later, when our children grow up, they might say, "Time is money" as if it were a normal assumption for everyone.

Now imagine an immigrant family with a young child from a cultural environment that does not teach competition for time entering our school system for the first time. After only one day of school, the child returns home and starts demanding time from her parents. Her parents ask, "Why are you so rude today? What did you learn in school?" The little child says, "I learned the letters A, B, and C. I learned to add and subtract. I played computer games and met a lot of new friends." She cannot tell her parents that she learned how to compete for time, because she did not learn it explicitly.

I would think none of us has ever heard a teacher in the United States says to a class in this way, "If you want to get an A, you have to learn to compete for time." We have never heard it; nonetheless, we all learned it. Competition for time is whispered through almost every classroom in the United States. There might be exceptions in which a teacher consciously decides not to teach competition and creates a cooperative learning environment. But the moment the students leave that classroom and move on to another classroom, "competition for time" is taught again and again, unconsciously and implicitly.

We bring these internal cultural elements unconsciously into our church. Collectively, we created the internal organizational culture of our church. Let us now look specifically at the internal organizational cultural of a church— the part of the iceberg that is submerged below the waterline and cannot be seen. They are the assumptions, values, patterns, and myths that are implicitly embedded in an organization, often below the consciousness of its members, but are key to the identity and operation of the community. Using the above example, a church in which most of the members were educated in the United States might believe with all their hearts that they should be inclusive of a particular ethnic group that has immigrated and settled in their neighborhood. In an effort to include them, the members invite them to come to a meeting so that they can explore ways to meet each other's needs in their community. During the meeting, the church members assume unconsciously that everyone knows how to compete for time and therefore speak freely about what is on their minds. As the meeting proceeds, they become more and more frustrated because their guests do not say anything or offer any suggestions. The meeting is a "waste of time" to them. Here, with all good intentions and even a great plan, but without the awareness of their internal culture, they are not able to realize their goal.

The internal culture includes the unconscious patterns that the community repeats continually. When confronted with the question why they do it, the reply is often, "We have always done it that way." There are implicit decision-making processes and unspoken rules based on deeply held values that are so deep that no one has articulated them for a long time. These processes also include informal leaders of the church. They are people who have no formal leadership roles; they are not on any committees, but they seem to have a great deal of influence in the decision-making of the church. The internal culture of a church also includes myths by which the community lives. Myths are stories that the community knew in the past but that through the generations most members have become unconscious of. These myths might revolve around particular personalities in the past, or traumatic experiences that were not dealt with constructively or worked through by the community. These myths might create an unconscious pattern that the church community keeps repeating and is not able to be free of until the myths become conscious again. Since we are unconscious of them, they are very hard to change. How do you change something that you don't know exists?

Upon examining its history, a church discovered that every time the church had to face the changing demographics around their neighborhood, they would start a building renovation project. This is a pattern they repeated for more than fifteen years. As a result, they had a beautiful church building with many halls and classrooms but with fewer and fewer people using the space. Also, they were financially drained; each church member gave more and more each year to support these building projects. Not until the church was able to expose this pattern were they able to break it and find a more constructive and relevant approach to their challenges in the future.

A minister came to me asking for help. She said, "I am really puzzled by what happened last week at my church. At our last church council meeting, the committee voted to hire a new gardener to take care of our grounds and the connecting cemetery. I thought everything was fine and that finally we were making some changes in the way we look to the community—a good-looking lawn and garden can go a long way in welcoming the people in our neighborhood. But then a week later, I saw a gardener working on the cemetery grounds and he was not the gardener that we had agreed to hire. It turned out that this stranger was the nephew of an old church member, Mr. Parish. I was shocked to find out that it was Mr. Parish who hired him to take care of the cemetery. Mr. Parish isn't even a member of the church council. What gave him the authority to do that?"

Upon further investigation, she discovered that Mr. Parish was the great-grandson of the founding minister of the church. The cemetery sits on the original site of the first church building. His great-grandfather laid the first stone of the original building, of which the foundation still can be seen. The cemetery had always been taken care of by one of the "original" family members.

Not until the myth behind this implicit decision making was revealed could the congregation have the chance to change that pattern. Everybody knew the story, but nobody talked about it anymore. It turned out that nothing could be decided without Mr. Parish's approval in that church.

In order to facilitate deep and profound change in any organization, we have to first explore and reveal what is in the internal culture, the submerged part of the iceberg. We cannot change something that we don't know is there or even exists. When we are able to expose the iceberg, we then have a choice. With conscious knowledge of the myths and patterns, we can decide whether we will continue to be controlled by these old patterns, assumptions, and myths or to find new patterns and frameworks with which to respond to the challenges that we face.

In the Process for Planned Change presented in this book, we spend a lot of time at the beginning of the process exploring the internal culture of the church organization. Exercises such as "Exploring the History of a Congregation," "Is Your Church Ministry Balanced?"[5] and "A Dialogue Process: Focusing on Differences in Communication Styles,"[6] from my previous books, are most helpful in enabling people to explore and clarify some of the patterns and myths of their church. A most crucial step of the Process for Planned Change is moving from *concerns* to *issues*. This is precisely the step where we invite congregational leaders to dig into their organizational iceberg and discover the deep causes of the concerns they have collected. If a team cannot or will not dig deeper into their internal organizational culture, the resulting change-plan will only address their concerns on the surface and will not move their church toward profound transformation.

Once we expose what are our frameworks, patterns, assumptions, and myths, we are ready and able to change, but to what? What criteria do we use to discern which direction to take, or how and what to change? As Christians, our decision to change has to be hinged on the discernment of God's will. Therefore, parallel to the process of revealing the internal cultural iceberg, we must actively seek God's purpose. In the next chapter, we will explore this dimension of our change model.

---

[5]Law, *Inclusion,* pp. 125–30.
[6]Law, *The Bush Was Blazing,* pp. 154–57.

CHAPTER 5

Holy Change Is Re-conversion

While Peter was below in the courtyard, one of the servant-girls of the high priest came by. When she saw Peter warming himself, she stared at him and said, "You also were with Jesus, the man from Nazareth." But he denied it, saying, "I do not know or understand what you are talking about." And he went out into the forecourt. Then the cock crowed. And the servant-girl, on seeing him, began again to say to the bystanders, "This man is one of them." But again he denied it. Then after a little while the bystanders again said to Peter, "Certainly you are one of them; for you are a Galilean." But he began to curse, and he swore an oath, "I do not know this man you are talking about." At that moment the cock crowed for the second time. Then Peter remembered that Jesus had said to him, "Before the cock crows twice, you will deny me three times." And he broke down and wept.

(MARK 14:66–72)

What was going on in Peter's mind? At a distance he had followed Jesus, who was taken to the High Priest, who had assembled all of the chief priests, elders, and scribes. Obviously he cared about Jesus, having been his disciple. But he was also worried about his own survival. If Jesus, his teacher, were to be put to death for "blasphemy," surely he, Jesus' number one disciple, if discovered, would suffer the same fate. So he denied knowing Jesus three times. He started to "curse and [swear] an oath." When the cock crowed a second time, he remembered what Jesus had said, and then he broke down and wept. He remembered not only Jesus' prediction of his action but also all the things that Jesus had tried to teach him. He remembered when Jesus foretold his death and resurrection for the first time and how he reacted to Peter's assumption about what a messiah should be—a king, a priest and a prophet, not someone who would be killed like a criminal. And Jesus said to him, "Get behind me, Satan." He remembered when Jesus took him to the mountain, and he saw a vision of Moses and Elijah talking with Jesus, and how he wanted to make three dwellings, one for each of them. Now he understood the voice from the cloud that said, "This is my Son, the Beloved; listen to him!" He remembered how he was so embarrassed when Jesus insisted on washing his feet that night. This moment of betrayal when the cock crowed the second time finally brought all these things into focus at a most profound level.

All that time Jesus was trying to challenge Peter's assumptions about what a messiah should be. Each time he did that, he pushed him to dig deeper into his own assumptions and myths about his religion, his society, and the world. In that moment, when he felt so far away from Jesus in his betrayal, he also felt the closeness of Jesus—closer than ever before, because he finally understood who Jesus was as God had intended it. He finally understood that the messiah was not someone whom others would serve and honor, or someone who would grab and hold onto power and prestige in the world. A messiah was to be a servant to others. A messiah was someone who spoke and stood for justice, and acted with compassion. He finally understood, but it seemed to be too late. He saw how the world had distorted his vision of the Kingdom of God and how Jesus had tried to correct it. In the depth of his despair, he recognized the distinction between his view and Christ's view of reality. In the depth of his despair, he saw the light. He met Jesus for the first time. He rediscovered the truth—God. So he broke down and wept.

St. Timothy's church membership had been in decline for more than ten years. Most of its members were over sixty-five and were of European backgrounds. For five years they had actively tried to do something about their decline. They tried hiring a youth director and an outreach coordinator, they tried changing the music in their worship services, and they tried calling their regional denominational office for help, but nothing worked. When their last pastor left, the denomination recommended that they call a part-time interim pastor for a year to help them with the transition. During this year, the interim pastor consistently preached and taught that they had to die and let go before they could rise and find new life again. But they did not understand that message, at least not at the deeper level at which it needed to be heard. When the denominational office offered the Kaleidoscope Project during the Lenten/Easter period, they came with a team. In the three months following, they again explored the issues, digging into their organizational iceberg, to discover the real cause of their inability to grow. At each session of the training, with which I was involved, they were invited to study scriptures together and to ask the question, "What does God invite us to do, be, or change through the scriptures?" They always studied as well the lesson appointed for the upcoming Sunday, according to the Common Lectionary. Also, each session included the celebration of the eucharist, in which Christ's death and resurrection were recalled while bread was broken and wine blessed as all partook in the body and bood of Christ.

In the third session, which took place on the Saturday before Palm Sunday, the team was charged with the task of digging deeper into their iceberg to discover the underlying issues that they needed to address. Suddenly, I sensed the energy converging in the middle of the room where they were sitting. I went over and looked at the flip chart on which they had been writing down their thoughts. It read, "We are so busy trying to survive that we have forgotten to be faithful." A couple of the team members were weeping.

This was the moment of truth. In the depth of their exploration, they discovered how far away they were from what they were called to do. In that discovery, they made the distinction between what they wanted—which was to survive—and what God called them to do, which was to be faithful. In the depth of their despair, they met God. When they emerged out of the depths where they had encountered the holy, they set a goal and designed an action plan to "die." They were willing to let go of their power and control. They were ready to embrace the dying of their old way of thinking about church in order to be faithful. Their action-plan included engaging in a dialogue with a nearby growing Hispanic congregation of the same denomination. They had learned that the church building of the Hispanic congregation was too small for them. The two congregations would explore merging and eventually moving the larger congregation of mostly Hispanic members to St. Timothy's church building.

This constituted a major shift in assumptions and attitude toward what it means to be a church. The church members changed because they wanted to be faithful, and not because they wanted to survive. This process of change came from their willingness to enter into their cultural iceberg and dig deep into it to discover how they were not being faithful, and in the process discovering what it means to be faithful. The cock of truth crowed, and they remembered who they were as God's people who live in the world but are not of the world. And they broke down their old walls of assumptions, patterns, structure, and boundaries, and they wept. As God revealed to them in their self-exploration, they were re-converted. Real change, holy change would happen for them.

> The Greek root that underlies the word "revelation" means "to uncover." As we engage in generative learning, we uncover the hidden assumptions behind our usual ways of thinking and discover how these have limited and even distorted our view of reality. We simultaneously uncover a fresh, unexpected vision of reality that discloses the world as God intends it to be. The challenge is to uncover, to reveal, the essential meaning of our experiences as revelatory encounters with the Holy...To live in truthfulness is to strive continually to uncover the false assumptions into which we have been conditioned by our social world and which distort our ability to mirror the good news revealed in Jesus Christ.[1]

This revelation is what makes the Christian change process different from all the other models of change in the world. It is recognizing what and who we are, and deciding to die to it so that a new form, new ideas, and new life can emerge, according to not our will, but God's will. Let me summarize the last two chapters and present more clearly the model of change on which the Process for Planned Change is based. There are four steps.

1. Delve into and reveal the internal organizational culture.
2. Discern actively the will of God.
3. Differentiate between our way and God's way.
4. Decide to follow God.

Let us describe these steps (the 4 D's) with more detail in practical terms. The first two steps need to happen simultaneously.

---

[1] Thomas R. Hawkins, *The Learning Congregation—A New Vision of Leadership* (Louisville: Westminster John Knox Press, 1997), p. 24.

I like to think of these two steps as being intertwined.

1. Delve into and reveal the internal organizational culture.

This is the invitation to dig deep down into our cultural iceberg to reveal its patterns, assumptions, and myths. All the activities suggested at the end of the last chapter will help in this step. The key question is: What caused us to behave and think the way we did? In the Process for Planned Change, this is the step through which we move from Concerns to Issues. A second way to explore what is in our organizational iceberg is by comparing our iceberg with another church's iceberg.

In the Kaleidoscope Projects that we have implemented in Vancouver, B.C., New York, and Oklahoma in which we utilized the Process for Planned Change, we invited teams of five to seven people from ten to fifteen congregations to come together for three to five monthly all-day training sessions. An important side effect of this approach was that these congregational teams also saw and heard what other teams were discovering in their organizations' icebergs. Some things were different, but some were similar. Since we always made sure that at least one-third of the teams were from fairly healthy congregations, the comparison among the congregational teams enabled each team to discern more clearly the patterns, assumptions, and myths that were embedded in their church community. I would recommend working through the process of this book with a neighboring church, so that you not only support each other's struggle but also can benefit from the comparison of each other's discoveries.

2. Discern actively the will of God.

In the Kaleidoscope Project, each time we gather, we always study the scriptures appointed for the upcoming Sunday, according to the Common Lectionary. The last question of each Bible study session is always: "What does God invite you to do, change, or be through this passage?" This is the principal way that we actively discern the will of God.

I would caution you not to choose a Bible passage to study that matches the theme of the meeting. If you do, you might be unconsciously manipulating the process by using the Bible to prove your point of view, rather than allowing God to speak through the scripture as it inspires those gathered.

I would recommend that you consistently set aside time (at least thirty minutes) at each meeting of your team to study scripture using the Community Bible Study Process.[2] This method is not an expert-based Bible study process. It is simply a discipline of reading scriptures together and inviting all persons to share their insights into how the particular scripture of the day informs and connects with their own and their organization's experiences and contexts.

The second method to actively discern God's will is to frame every gathering and meeting as a worship service. The full-day training should always end with the celebration of communion. A three-hour meeting should be framed as an evening prayer service. In our thanksgiving, prayers, and liturgical actions, we are continually reminded of the centrality of our faith, the gospel. This is essential in supporting the struggle that we might have in doing step one—delving into our own internal culture. The constant reminder of the gospel will give us courage to explore deeper and further, knowing that God is with us even at our darkest moments.

3. Differentiate between our way and God's way

When we faithfully and deliberately intertwine the first two steps of our change process, eventually we will find ourselves at a point deep in our exploration where we will feel frustrated and perhaps even lost. Like Peter in the gospel story, and the change team from St. Timothy's, in the depth of our despair we might hear a cock crowing a second time. And suddenly everything makes sense. Suddenly we understand all the gospel lessons that we have been listening to over the

---

[2]Law, *The Wolf Shall Dwell with the Lamb*, pp. 121–31.

months. This is the moment when we can differentiate between our assumptions and God's will; our patterns and God's way; our myths and the divine myth, the gospel; our vision of the world and God's realm. We see how we have strayed from God and how far away we are from God. In this ability to make the differentiation, we find God revealed to us. We can see God more clearly. In the revelation of God, we are faced with a decision to choose.

> "Today...I have set before you life and death, blessings and curses. Choose life so that you and your descendants may live." (Deuteronomy 30:19–20)

4. Decide to follow God.

We have submerged ourselves in our murky water, and we have discovered not only our own distorted reality, but God, face-to-face. We have to decide now; we have to choose whether to continue to hold on to our old frameworks and patterns, or to follow God. When we decide to follow God, we are turned around, we repent, and we are re-converted again to be Christ's own. Then there are new possibilities, new hopes, and new life. The new creation that we yearned for before is now becoming clearer and closer to reality.

The fundamental difference between the secular change process and our change process is that we are not the ones who make change happen or impose change on others. The principal actor in our change process is God. Our role is to create a gracious time and space for members of our community to delve into its organization iceberg while actively discerning the will of God. It is through the revelation of God to the members of the community in the first two steps that the conversion—holy change—takes place.

Holy change is a deep and profound change that stems from the conversion of the heart when we finally decide to choose God. The changes in our behavior and patterns are more than just changes on the surface; they are expressions of the profound transformation that has taken place deep inside us. We act differently, not because it is popular or fashionable; rather, we act differently because we have reconnected with God through Christ again. Our changes become holy. Our actions are then sacred. They are the outward expression of the inward grace that we have experienced.

> I will sprinkle clean water upon you, and you shall be clean from all your uncleannesses, and from all your idols I will cleanse you. A new heart I will give you, and a new spirit I will put within you; and I will remove from your body the heart of stone and give you a heart of flesh. (Ezekiel 36: 25–26)

CHAPTER 6

What Shape Is Your Church In?

For five years I have tested and modified many times the change model and theory presented in this book. Each modification has been based on evaluations and feedback from congregation teams that have worked through the process. Most of the time, the model became more effective after each modification. Since I was so intimately involved in the evolution of the model, I found it very hard to describe the model objectively and to articulate the reasons why it worked. Therefore, it was a joy to discover a new set of vocabulary and images, provided by other writers and researchers on organizational change, that could actually help me describe this model and why it works.

While I was researching this book I came across a book called *The End of Change* in which the authors described four types of organizations using four geometrical shapes: Pyramid,

Cube, Cylinder, and Sphere.[1] They illustrated how each of these organizations dealt with change effectively by creating a stable structure in which innovation could be accommodated. In very neutral terms, they proposed that each company should recognize its operational style/shape and maximize its strength while avoiding what they called "change fatigue" by minimizing turbulence and resistance. If staying with the same operating style fails to meet the market change, then a movement to change shape might be required.

Even though churches are structurally smaller and less complicated than the organizations that these authors described, I found that by applying these images to describe churches, we can understand better why some churches make changes with ease and grace while other churches cannot, no matter how much help they receive.

"A Pyramid is the most difficult structure to move. It sits solidly on its broad base and is difficult to rock. The only way to move it is by nudging it along, but there's a lot of resistance. It's hard, perhaps impossible to move  it very far very fast."[2] Most churches function like a Pyramid. They like to "maintain stability in an environment of incremental innovation, following a strategy of slow adaptation and occasional avoidance."[3] They dislike discontinuous change involving high levels of innovation that challenge their core assumptions, myths, and patterns. If a challenge is too far from its traditions, they will do anything to avoid or disable it. If they change, they tend to want to build on their tried-and-true traditions a little bit at a time. They will simply repeat old patterns that have worked before, such as developing a better stewardship program, starting a youth program, changing the

[1]Peter Scott-Morgan, Erik Hoving, Henk Smit, and Arnoud Van Der Slot, *The End of Change* (New York: McGraw Hill, 2001), pp. 1–34.
[2]Ibid., p. xv.
[3]Ibid., p. xiv.

leadership, hiring outreach workers, and so on. A church in this form tends to have many circular patterns repeating over and over to reinforce the foundation of the Pyramid.

On occasion, a Pyramid might construct a smaller Pyramid next door to handle the changes in their environment without having to challenge the core myths, assumptions, and patterns of the original large Pyramid.[4] Many denominations use this method to start "ethnic" ministries and "nest" them in existing English-speaking congregations. For example, an English-speaking church might welcome a growing Korean ministry of the same denomination to worship in their church building. This is done with the approval of the church leadership and also supported by the regional denominational leaders. Their hope is that eventually the two congregations will integrate into one big multicultural church. In many cases, when the Korean ministry grows to be a viable community with its own Pyramid operation, instead of the two communities coming together, conflict begins to rear its ugly head. Eventually the Korean ministry might have to move out and find a new home elsewhere.

The strength of the Pyramid model is that it is stable; many church denominations and local congregations have enjoyed many years of stability operating this way. However, the Pyramid is too slow to react and often too easily threatened by a world full of fast and profound challenges.

"A Cube is also stable, firmly on its base. To move it you push it [in] just the right place and get it to pivot on its edge. Keep applying the pressure and it will roll over into a new position. To move it more, you need to apply pressure once again, pivot it up, and keep pushing until it rolls over."[5] Some churches behave like Cubes. They are able to go through major profound

---

[4]Ibid., p. 4.
[5]Ibid., p. xv.

changes in between periods of stability. They "maximize periods of stability by clustering spasmodic innovation into short, efficient bursts."[6] This approach to change is often linear. The goal is to move the organization from one state to another with careful preparation and well-thought-out timing. Many churches intentionally move through this kind of change process when their pastor retires or moves on and they have to call a new one. Many denominations use the interim ministry model or a transition consultant to enable a community to make this kind of "cubic" change before they call a new pastor.

Some churches start a major self-study every three to five years in order to make sure the church stays lively and responsive to the community in which they reside. They may arrive at a new mission focus and an action plan to move toward this new vision with clearly stated milestones. Members of a best-practice Cube-like church actually are used to this periodic major change and are very receptive and ready to do it. When the time comes to make the major move, the whole church membership will be ready emotionally, practically, and spiritually, and tip over the Cube, landing squarely on its new vision and direction for ministry.

The strength of the churches that operate like a Cube is that with careful planning and preparation, they can accomplish profound and faithful change with great innovations. The weakness of a Cube is that it cannot do this quickly. The time and energy it takes to study, develop a new vision, and plan how to get everyone on board are high and intensive. In a fast-paced, turbulent world, the Cube often takes too long to make the change. After great effort, when the Cube finally tips over onto its new state, the world has changed again.

"The Sphere, of course, is relatively easy to move in any direction and can be steered as it is rolled. Change the direction as often as you like. Compared with the other structures, it's

---

[6]Ibid., p. 12.

highly mobile."[7] Very few of our churches respond to challenges as if they were Spheres, which "reduce disruption by developing the maximum number of options for responding to

environmental changes. The key words are assessment and action."[8] A good church-start often utilizes this model, under which the fledgling church might initiate a number of potential ministry projects. The assessment of these various projects after a period of time will give the church developers data pointing to which projects might be most effective in that particular ministry site. These projects might become the foundation of the new church plan. Some large churches may also operate as Spheres. With their large budgets, they can initiate and support a number of different ministry projects at the same time. These projects could go in many different directions, often with different emphases and varying degrees of success. Sometimes the leadership might discern that one of the projects seems to be the most promising and to offer a timely ministry; then the whole church will put their energy into moving in that direction for a period of time.

The weakness of a Sphere is that it might move according to whichever is the strongest force pushing it, without a clear sense of purpose and focus. For example, I knew a small congregation in a high-need neighborhood. Every time a new group of people expressed a need, the church would rush into action to serve them. It took the church members a long time to realize that when they rushed to one group's service, the other ministry projects they had started suffered. They just did not have enough resources and energy to do them all. Consequently, they found themselves working harder and harder, yet they were not getting any significant result in any

[7]Ibid., p. xv.
[8]Ibid., p. 28.

of the ministry projects. The Sphere model needs clearly stated principles, values, and criteria with which to assess the various options available before taking action, or else it will roll all over the place.

"A Cylinder, on the other hand, is easy to move, so long as it's rolling on its long axis. Try pushing the cylinder in any other direction and it's nearly as difficult as shoving at a Pyramid or Cube. Once the Cylinder is rolling, you can gently steer it—but only gradually."[9] Few of our churches are like the Cylinder, which "minimize[s] disruption by building repetitive  [innovation] into their process. The key words are efficiency and learning."[10] Repetitive innovation processes are taught and practiced in all the different functioning components of the church. Even though Cylinder-like churches are changing constantly, people find stability and safety in the cyclical repetitive processes. They have learned and practice these cyclical processes through which they can simply "roll in" the new challenges that come their way. The challenge might be different every time, but the process more or less stays the same. Each time the community moves through a cycle of activities, it evolves into something different when it comes around to the other side.

Mutual Invitation is one of these effective cyclical processes. When there is a new person, even with a very different background, joining the group, Mutual Invitation automatically includes the person by simply inviting that person to share along with everyone else, without putting that person on the spot or ignoring the person. At the end of the process, having listened to the new person's needs and perspective, the group

---

[9]Ibid., p. xv.
[10]Ibid., p. 20.

might decide to adjust its community operation in order to truly welcome the new member.

The strength of the Cylinder is that it can respond to rapid change efficiently. When the cycle of activities includes exploration of new ideas, outside input, internal analysis, and learning, the church comes out of the cycle able to respond to the challenge quickly and with innovations. Its weakness is that if we do not apply the right pressure in the appropriate places, the Cylinder may stubbornly roll in one direction only and therefore be unable to change direction, even when it is necessary. When we do that, we are reverting to the Pyramid, reducing our cyclical process into a fixed circular pattern, and reinforcing the broad foundation of its base, thereby resisting any innovative challenges.

Let me offer a quick way for us to recognize how these different shape-churches function. A member of a church challenges the church to explore reaching out to a different cultural group that has settled in their neighborhood. A Pyramid-church would react by asking, "Are they like us?" and then, "What can we do that we always have done better in order to attract this new group?" A Cube-church would start a study group that would report back to the church what this new group was like, what their needs were, and so forth. Then they would set up another committee to create a three-year plan to help the church reach out to this group. A Sphere-church would say, "Why not? Let's do that too." A Cylinder-church would use a cyclical process that they had used before, such as inviting the person who issued this challenge to share his or her ideas. They would listen and pray and then decide what they needed to do. When newcomers from the differing cultural group came to their church, they would simply invite these newcomers to come to their small groups, in which these cyclical processes were being used, to include them right away.

According to the researchers who put forth this "shape" theory, there is a linear migration pattern (with one exception: from Cube to Pyramid) that evokes the least disruption and resistance.[11] (See Figure 6.1.) Skipping one or more shapes would be met with great resistance. The only exception is the move from a Cube back to a Pyramid. All the Cube needs to do is to get comfortable and not implement another new change initiative, and thereby let the stable structure settle into the Pyramid. The reverse is more difficult, especially for churches. Once a church settles into its repeated pattern for a longer period of time, its members may forget how to initiate major changes and may actively resist them.

Figure 6.1

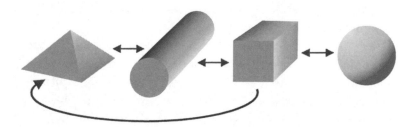

For example, a church had a very healthy history of dealing with change like a Cube. However, the last pastor stayed for 20 years, and for the last fifteen years did not help the congregation to make any change initiatives. When the pastor retired, the church membership was in decline for five years. When the denominational office sent a consultant to help the church members deal with this transition, they were not able to respond constructively to the suggestion of change in order to meet the new challenges in their neighborhood.

Much of congregational development work has to do with moving a church from being a Pyramid to a Cube so that it can make the essential paradigm shift. Changing from a maintenance model to a missionary model is just one example of the profound change or shift of paradigm required. The

---

[11]Ibid., pp. 277–93.

concept of "paradigm shift" has been around since the 1980s—at least that was when I learned about it. My experience has shown me that getting a church to change its paradigm is extremely difficult. It takes time, patience, and repeated effort. The shape theory helps explain why. In order for this fundamental shift in paradigm to take place, we are asking many churches that have been operating like Pyramids to roll over like Cubes.

One of the most difficult transitions that many churches have had to make is to learn how to grow beyond 200 active members. Researchers have shown that in order for the church to do that, its church members have to make a major shift in their understanding of church organization—from a Pastoral church (50–150 Sunday attendance) to a Program church (150–350 Sunday attendance).[12] The Pastoral church has its focus on the pastoral relationship between the pastor and the church members. The pastor is at the center of everything. The pastoral church model only works when the church has between 50 and 150 active members. When the church grows beyond 150 and is moving toward the 200 range, the pastoral approach will cease to be effective, because it is physically impossible for one pastor to maintain a close pastoral relationship with that many people. If the church is to grow beyond 150 successfully, its members must learn to accept a new way of experiencing and organizing the church.

The Program church has its focus on offering programs in which its members can participate. A member's primary relationship to the church is through the particular program in which he or she is involved. The pastor's role is no longer primarily in the pastoral relationship with everyone but in empowering, supporting, and training the leaders of the various programs. Sometimes the pastor also takes on the administrative

---

[12]Arlin J. Rothauge, *Sizing Up a Congregation for New Member Ministry* (New York: The Domestic and Foreign Missionary Society, 1995), pp. 15–30. This booklet can be ordered through Episcopal Parish Services, P.O. Box 1321, Harrisburg, PA 17105.

role in managing these programs if the church does not have a church administrator.

With the shape theory presented in this chapter, we now understand why it is so difficult to move a church from thinking and behaving like a Pastoral church to thinking and behaving like a Program church. If the church is already functioning like a Cube—that is, its members are used to periodic major changes and visioning processes—this proposal to move to a new paradigm of being a Program church in order to grow would be an easy one to accept. I have seen churches that, with careful planning, have made this move with ease and excitement. If the church has been functioning as a Cylinder, the transition is still relatively easy. All it needs to do is to slow down one of the cyclical change processes. Again, with careful planning and timing, a Cylinder-like church can shift to being a Cube for a period of time in order to make this major shift in patterns and assumptions.

However, if the church has been functioning as a Pyramid, this move is much more difficult and can be met with great resistance. This is why we have the "200" barrier. In order to do this, one must first move the Pyramid-like church toward becoming a Cylinder by transforming the existing circular patterns of the Pyramid into cyclical change processes. These cyclical processes will increase the community's ability to deal constructively with new information, new challenges, and new ideas. We might need to train leaders to use these cyclical processes and start implementing them in as many parts of the community as possible. When more and more parts of the congregation's components are functioning like Cylinders, then the congregation might be more ready for a major shift in paradigm (such as a Cube) at a later time.

It is even more difficult to move from a Pyramid to a Sphere, which involves moving through two intermediate states. For example, I used to utilize a Sphere-like problem-solving process. The process involved looking at all the options available. Then, we would explore and try to understand each option. Before deciding, we first developed a set of criteria based on our values and beliefs. Using these criteria as a guide, we could select the option that would meet most of our criteria. In doing so, the choice that we made would most likely be able to solve our problem. My experience with this process is that it only works when the church, like a Cube, has experienced periodic change before. Church members can fully explore these options without the fear of losing their identity and security because they know, as part of a Cube-like organization, that eventually they will settle into a new, stable structure. Therefore, moving temporarily to function like a Sphere is acceptable. However, when a church has been operating like a Pyramid, any suggestions to look at options other than what they are "used to" will be dismissed as impossible and unimaginable. The Sphere-like approach to change seems too fast and chaotic to them.

I believe most of our churches are still functioning like Pyramids. Yet, most of the changes that we would like our churches to make require the church to function like a Cube or sometimes even like a Sphere. No wonder we have such a difficult time trying to help our churches to change! The shape theory points out that in order to help our Pyramid-like churches to consider change, we first have to move them into the intermediate state of the Cylinder. This is the most important step, which was missing in the past. Even for churches that are already functioning like a Cube, with the rapid rate of change around us, the Cube approach requires too much time and energy. The resulting change might be too slow. Again, this points to the need to move the Cube back to a Cylinder so that it can deal with rapid challenges more effectively in between major change initiatives.

In order for the church to stay effective and faithful in a rapidly changing world, I propose that we must help our churches to oscillate between functioning like a Cylinder and like a Cube. To be able to address deep and fast challenges, the church must be quick like a Cylinder to absorb and address the fast-paced challenges and changes, but occasionally be able to make a necessary major shift in order to change direction like a Cube.

George Parsons and Speed Leas suggested that a healthy congregation should be able to live in the creative tension between order and freedom.

> Because the forces of order and freedom are constantly in tension in congregational life, we would posit that healthy congregational systems will create tension— to maintain internal variety and stay flexible and open to renewal. Again, the healthy system moves along the continuum but is not stagnant and "balanced." A healthy congregation lives with certain kinds of contention created by the voices from both sides. We would argue that unless there are ongoing reasons for a congregational system to contend, unless there are opportunities to exercise these tensions, the congregation will lose its flexibility and experience decline. Without reasons to contend, congregations will either experience the excesses of order (which become overcontrol) or the excesses of freedom (which lead to chaos). One set of excesses is not preferred over the other. Either can kill a congregation.[13]

If we superimpose this order-freedom continuum on our shape theory, on the "order" side is the Pyramid and on the "freedom" side is the Sphere. To live in the tension in which there is a balance of the two extremes, we need to enable our congregation to operate mostly like a Cylinder and occasionally like a Cube. The Cylinder approach maintains a sense of order by utilizing repeated cyclical change processes. Built into the cyclical processes are the opportunities for the congregation

---

[13]George Parsons and Speed B. Leas, *Understanding Your Congregation as A System* (The Alban Institute, 1993), pp. 22–23.

to learn and to address new challenges that might lead to small but innovative changes. Occasionally, the healthy congregation moves into operating like a Cube and might even consider various options like a Sphere, and thereby make a profound change in the life of the community. In this way, a congregation can benefit from opportunities and new ideas from the chaos and freedom side of the continuum but also return to the somewhat orderly Cylinder structure.

Figure 6.2

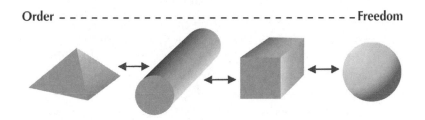

Order –Freedom

When congregations live between order and freedom, not allowing the excesses of either to dominate, an atmosphere is created in which different voices and approaches are honored. The tension becomes something life-giving, creative, and renewing, as the "internal variety" encourages the benefits of both order and freedom.[14]

The Episcopal Diocese of Texas, under the leadership of Bishop Claude E. Payne since 1995, has successfully moved the majority of its congregations from a maintenance understanding of church to what he calls a "missionary model." This shift has resulted in significant increases in attendance, baptisms, and stewardship in five years. This is how he describes this model:

---

[14]Ibid., p. 22.

The missionary model is at once evolutionary and revolutionary. It entails a dramatic shift in perspective and focus, and yet it feels familiar…It is the combination of the proven and the innovative that creates a contemporary missionary Church designed for the New Apostolic Age.[15]

In order to enable the diocese to embody this missionary model of ministry, Bishop Payne reorganized its operational structure to align with its missionary purpose. He called this structure the "spoke-and-wheel" management model. The rim of the wheel is the "missionary outposts," the congregations. The hub is the bishop and the diocesan staff. The spokes are the lines of communication and decision-making. The significant characteristics of this management model as different from the hierarchical pyramid are that the communication and decision-making are balanced and spread across the wheel. The action is at the outer rim of the wheel where the congregations are. When the wheel is in motion, it creates "centrifugal force" and the energy is directed outward.[16]

Perhaps the reason why this management model worked to enable the Diocese of Texas to change is that it intentionally transformed the diocese from operating like a Pyramid to operating like a Cylinder. "The Bishop of Texas restructured the diocese by using elements that were largely in place. Therefore, his reorganization is not characterized as much by new elements as by a reordering of relationships among existing elements."[17] Using what is there from the old Pyramid structure, reorganizing it into a dynamic Cylinder (spoke-and-wheel) structure is the least threatening approach to change, and therefore the transition creates the least disturbance. Once the Cylinder is in place, with careful planning and timing, the

---

[15]Claude E. Payne and Hamilton Beazley, *Reclaiming the Great Commission* (San Francisco: Jossey-Bass, 2000), p. xii.

[16]Ibid., pp. 75–77.

[17]Ibid., p. 77.

movement toward a major shift in the direction of the missionary model of ministry for the whole diocese (the Cubic move) can be done over time with ease. The Diocese of Texas, with great care and detailed planning, did this through an event called "A Gathering of the Diocese: New Horizons, New Perspectives, New Disciples" to introduce this new paradigm to the majority of the diocese.[18] This is an example of creating tension between order and freedom by utilizing a combination of Cube and Cylinder processes in the middle of the continuum. The Cylinder provides the feel of the familiar—the evolutionary—and the Cube model moves the community toward the dramatic shift in perspective—to the revolutionary.

St. Mary's was a church stuck in the Pyramid mode of operation. The glory days of twenty years ago, when the church was full, were gone. The church suffered a steady decline for at least ten years. When I started working with the leaders of the church, the church could not afford a full-time pastor. In their maintenance/survival mode, they were blaming each other, especially their last pastor, who went on stress leave and swore never to go back. I was sent in by the denominational office to help this church deal with their "problems."

The denominational leaders and I knew that this church needed a change in the way its members understood church, a shift from a maintenance to a missionary model. In other words, it needed a paradigm shift from being a Pyramid to being a Cube. I also knew that if I walked in and started explaining this need to change, they would simply shut down and resist. In fact, the denominational leaders had tried instructing each new pastor they sent to this church that her or his job was to help the congregation make this shift. However, one after another, the pastors got little result. This was because moving from a Pyramid to a Cube was too big and too discontinuous a transition for St. Mary's.

---

[18]Ibid., pp. 62–73.

My first meeting with the leaders of St. Mary's was carefully designed, with cyclical elements and processes that I could repeat. Here is the outline:

1. Opening prayers.
2. Presentation of the Respectful Communication Guidelines.
3. Study one of the upcoming lectionary Bible lessons using Mutual Invitation as a technique to help each member to share reflections.
4. A presentation or a process to explore an area of concern to the church. For example, presentation of the average Sunday attendance for the last fifteen years in graphic form, presentation of the demographic information about their neighborhood according to the Census Data, drawing a picture depicting the decision-making structure of the church, and so forth.
5. Discuss a related topic using Mutual Invitation.
6. Summary of learning and discovery.
7. Closing circle prayers.

For a whole year we met monthly, and each time we utilized the same meeting format. We studied a different Bible passage according to the seasons of the church year and explored a different issue/topic. Most importantly, we consistently practiced Mutual Invitation as the primary form of sharing. I used the repeated parts of the meeting format and the cyclical processes to provide a sense of order and stability. The exploration of a new topic each time was there to help the church to dig deeper into their organizational cultural iceberg. Each time we moved through this cyclical process, we moved deeper into discovering the unconscious assumptions, myths, and patterns of the church. Like a spiral acting as a screw, we drilled deeper and deeper each time we met. Over time, we finally found the courage to reveal explicitly the following pattern of the church's decision-making process. A few people had always dominated the decision making of the church.

When they did not get their way, they would threaten to leave, and the rest of the members would beg them to return. The major drops in attendance every five years or so in their past were caused by these few strong personalities who refused to compromise with people who disagreed with them. Even though there were other long-time members who were ready to make real changes, their voices were not heard and were often shut out by those few dominant personalities. As we moved through the cyclical processes, such as the Mutual Invitation Process, at each meeting, the voices of the silent ones were heard for the first time in many years. Each time the Bible passage was read, everyone, independent of their role in the church, was invited to share her or his insights and interpretations.

After one year of meeting in the Cylinder form, the church was facing a major decision regarding music in the Sunday services. Instead of going through the old pattern in which the same few people dominated the decision, the whole church got involved in the process. Without being coached, they designed their meeting using the same format that I had taught them. With everyone's voice being heard, they decided to purchase the new denominational hymnal and would learn at least one new hymn each Sunday. While they were making this decision, one of the power-holders from the old Pyramid structure threatened to leave. This time, the rest of the church members did not run after this person to beg him to come back as they had the many times before. They made a conscious decision not to go through the old pattern again. With renewed confidence in their ability to change things, they started a welcome-the-newcomers program. Each time a new person or family came to church, within a week they would receive a visit from a team of church members presenting a gift basket of bread, fruits, and flowers from the church garden. The whole church voted to support this change initiative, with little resistance this time. Within three months, St. Mary's was retaining new members for the first time in fifteen years.

The church has a great potential to operate like a Cylinder, because so many things that the church does are cyclical in nature. Our weekly worship is cyclical. Each time the format stays almost the same but the content differs, depending on the scriptural passage being used, the preacher, and the major events happening in the community and the world that week. Our annual church calendar is cyclical in nature. Each year, we start with Advent around December, then we move through Christmas and Epiphany. We enter Lent around February and then Holy Week and Easter, followed by Pentecost.

However, not all cyclical processes are "cylindrical," as described here. Many of our churches go through their circular patterns, each time stubbornly holding on to the same rules and patterns, without either learning or innovating. They do the same sorts of things with the same people each time as a way of ensuring their stability and security. These kinds of circular patterns are but expressions of the Pyramid organization described earlier. In order for our cyclical process to be effective in addressing change, it must involve learning and result in some innovation, however small. In Christian terms, our cyclical processes must be full of grace.

- **G**racious
- **R**eflective
- **A**daptable
- **C**hrist-centered
- **E**mpowering

The cyclical processes must enable us to be **gracious** to each other. They must provide room for each person to share perspectives, ideas, and feelings without the fear of being judged. They must support each person to extend his or her boundary to consider others' perspectives and experiences. These cyclical processes must also invite us to be **reflective** about who we are as individuals and as a community. Each time we go through such a process, we should come around to learning more about our internal culture, and digging deeper into our individual and organization cultural iceberg. These cyclical processes must be **adaptable** to different contexts and situations. We should be able to employ these processes again and again without feeling that we are repeating ourselves. They should be like liturgy—forms that we use every time we worship; but because of the different hymns, scriptures, and people in the liturgy, each worship experience is different and has new meaning. For example, we learn something new each time we use the Mutual Invitation process, because the people and the subject are different. These processes must be **Christ-centered,** in that they must constantly keep us focused on God's will. Being Christ-centered will enable us to make the crucial turning point when it comes to choosing between our old way or God's way. Finally, these cyclical processes must be **empowering,** in that they must empower each person to speak from the heart authentically. More importantly, these cyclical processes must enable the formerly voiceless to be heard. For the voice of Christ sometimes comes from the smallest amongst us.

Some of the grace-filled cyclical processes that I have used regularly are:

1. Mutual Invitation
2. Respectful Communication Guidelines
3. Community Bible Study
4. Regularized Meeting Format
5. Circle Prayer
6. Songs sung at each gathering

When I utilized an earlier form of the Process for Planned Change, I was frustrated that, while the concept was sound, I could not get the churches and ministry groups to work through it with significant positive results. This was because the Process for Planned Change, in itself, is just another change process that challenges a church organization to make a shift in paradigm. When we started teaching the church members to use these grace-filled cyclical processes regularly while they worked through the Process for Planned Change, we observed a marked difference in our results. By the time they moved deeper into discerning what was in their organizational iceberg, they had learned from these processes that change was possible and that faithful change and learning could be beneficial and energizing. The turning point came when they had to choose between God's way and their ways, a shift in paradigm. They were more receptive to it.

When we roll the planning process in together with the grace-filled cyclical processes, we turn the Process for Planned Change into a grace-filled cyclical process as well. Chapter 9 contains Suggested Agenda for each session of the Process for Planned Change. Each session is designed with a similar format utilizing essential grace-filled cyclical processes and skills. Also, there are two major segments in each agenda: the Diversity Training and the Planning Segments. The Diversity Training Segment seeks to teach the team these inclusive cyclical processes and skills and to reinforce the importance of using these processes in their planning work. The Planning Segment moves the group through the Process for Planned Change step-by-step. When all the pieces come together in the dynamic, cylindrical form, new life emerges. The resulting change is holy and the action sacred.

CHAPTER 7

Whenever Two or Three Are Gathered in Christ, Something Will Change

When [Jesus] returned to Capernaum after some days, it was reported that he was at home. So many gathered around that there was no longer room for them, not even in front of the door; and he was speaking the word to them. Then some people came, bringing to him a paralyzed man, carried by four of them. And when they could not bring him to Jesus because of the crowd, they removed the roof above him; and after having dug through it, they let down the mat on which the paralytic lay. When Jesus saw their faith, he said to the paralytic, "Son, your sins are forgiven." Now some of the scribes were sitting there, questioning in their hearts, "Why does this fellow speak in this way? It is blasphemy! Who can forgive sins but God alone?" At once Jesus perceived in his spirit that they were discussing these questions among themselves; and he said to them, "Why do you raise such questions in your hearts? Which is easier, to say to the paralytic,

*'Your sins are forgiven,' or to say, 'Stand up and take your mat
and walk'? But so that you may know that the Son of Man has
authority on earth to forgive sins"—he said to the paralytic—
"I say to you, stand up, take your mat and go to your home."
And he stood up, and immediately took the mat and went out
before all of them; so that they were all amazed and glorified
God, saying, "We have never seen anything like this!"*

(MARK 2:1–12)

People often ask me, "How do you begin to get a congregation to enter this transformation process?" I always turn to the biblical passage cited above. This is the only account of a healing story that involved the help of a group of people. Four people dug through the roof of a house and lowered a paralyzed man on a mat in order to present this man to Jesus. What persistence and dedication these friends had! This passionate insistence that their paralyzed friend be placed in front of Christ was perhaps what Jesus affirmed as their faith. And their faith facilitated the beginning of healing, and holy change.

The transformation of a church community often requires a group of faithful members who are willing to bring their community's paralysis to a place where Christ dwells, where God's grace is abundant, and where the Word is spoken and lived. For some communities that are stuck in the Pyramid mode of operation, a group of faithful members might have to do extraordinary things—like digging through a roof—in order to enter a grace-filled environment and begin this healing process. They must be willing to commit their time and energy, and, most importantly, be persistent.

The traditional consulting model usually involves a consultant working directly with a church for a period of time. The consultant's job is to take the church through a change process. If the consultant is successful, he or she will leave the church in a new, changed state. If the consultant is not effective, after she or he leaves, the church might simply revert to where things have always been. Nothing changes. When I was working for the Diocese of New Westminster as the Ministry and Congregation Development Officer, the demand for consulting support was so high that the traditional one-consultant–one-church model was not going to work. I had to find a better way to use my time and energy. Instead of working with one church at a time, I recruited ten congregations to send a team of five to seven people to come to five full-day training sessions over a period of five months. In this format, I still functioned as a consultant, but I was one step removed from working with the churches directly. Instead, I trained a team of faithful members to return to their churches to implement the change process. I will share my experience in working with these teams in order to show how this process works.

In the first session, after explaining what the programs entailed, we invited the members of each team to sign a covenant committing themselves to the five training sessions. Usually the teams that signed the covenant consisted of people who already had some idea that their church needed to change. If the teams were not ready, they would not sign the covenant, nor would we pressure them into doing so. For the teams that remained, we took great care to create a grace-filled environment each time the training session convened.

"And [Jesus] was speaking the Word to them."

The first step to creating a grace-filled environment is to create a place where the Word of Christ is spoken and lived. We needed to let the teams know that they had brought their problems to the right place—the home of Jesus. We created this place where the Word was spoken through the discipline of studying scriptures together. We took great care in designing each training session using a similar pattern based on our Anglican liturgy. For example, the eucharist was always celebrated at the end of each session. Each time we met, we presented and discussed the Respectful Communication Guidelines in order to ensure mutual respect throughout the day. In this place, we taught them cyclical processes that were gracious, reflective, adaptable, Christ-centered, and empowering. As they dug into their organization's cultural iceberg, we consistently asked them the following questions: "Where is God in all this?" "How does God invite you to change and do?" "How can Christ be at the heart of your planning process?" They were also instructed to use these processes in their own local team meetings. By the third training session, all the teams were beginning to see the effect these cyclical processes had on their team interactions. Some had even tried these processes at work and at home and found them to be very useful in empowering everyone's voices.

"Which is easier, to say to the paralytic, 'Your sins are forgiven,' or to say, 'Stand up and take your mat and walk'?"

In this rhetorical question, Jesus showed those who were questioning in their hearts that he was not only addressing the external physical curing of the paralysis. More importantly, he was dealing with the deeper, profound issue that caused the paralysis in the first place. The healing was not just correcting the external mechanical challenge; rather, the healing dealt with an internal transformation. This internal transformation could not happen in our church communities unless we revealed the deeper, sometimes unconscious, patterns, assumptions, and myths that caused their paralysis. In our change process, having provided the teams with a grace-filled environment and increased their capacity to reflect and dig into their church systems, we had enabled them to be ready to delve deeper into their organization's iceberg.

> People start discussing "undiscussable" subjects only when they develop the reflection and inquiry skills that enable them to talk openly about complex, conflictive issues without invoking defensiveness.

People start seeing and dealing with interdependencies and deeper causes of problems only as they develop the skills of systems thinking.[1]

This was the crucial turning point of the Process for Planned Change, in which we invited the teams to name their churches' issues. When they were able to do that, the transformation and healing would begin.

"Take your mat and go to your home."

Then the teams were asked to take what they learned and go home. They knew what the issues were by this time. With their own healing and empowerment, they now could help their home church communities to move through this transformation. We taught them how to set concrete, achievable goals based on the issues that they named. From the goals they had set, they then created action plans that they would take back and implement in their home churches. Members of the teams were motivated because they had learned and practiced skills and processes that had given them personal results. They also learned that they were not alone. There were other committed people in their own teams who took this change process seriously. There also were other church teams around them who supported their struggle in the training sessions. They were now ready to take their action plans back and help their home communities to move through this transformation.

One might ask, "What can a small group of people do in a church that has had a long history of denial and resistance to change?" We thought about that when we designed the first Kaleidoscope Project in both New York and Vancouver. We observed the teams as they set their goals, created their action plans, and then implemented their plans. A few of the congregational teams discovered that their congregations had

---

[1]Peter Senge, *The Dance of Change* (New York: Doubleday, 1999), p. 9.

dealt with change like a Cube before—they had periodically experienced profound changes. They then used the Process for Planned Change to carefully move their churches through this major change initiative. If their assessments were correct, they would be very successful in implementing their plans.

However, most of the congregational teams discovered that their congregations had a very ingrained Pyramid-type structure. Without the benefit of the theory developed in this book, they determined that before they could introduce any idea of profound change to their churches, they would first move them into functioning like Cylinders—practicing cyclical grace-filled processes. They designed plans that included teaching the cyclical processes in various places in their church; for example, in church council meetings, Bible study groups, adult education classes, and so forth.

Our experiences with providing annual training over a period of four years also affirmed this pattern. A number of teams thought their churches were ready for a major change but found out when they implemented their action plan that they were faced with major resistance. Some of the teams returned a second time to move through the Process for Planned Change. Their resulting action plans were more realistic and were more in line with the other teams' plan to propagate the cyclical processes as a preparation to a later, more profound change. Perhaps when they move through the Process for Planned Change cycle for yet a third time on their own, they may be ready to embark on a deeper, more profound change.

In this model of change, we do not try to change the whole system. That is close to impossible. We start with a group of committed people. We teach them the cyclical processes that enable them to address change, deal with differences, and empower all the voices involved. We then plant this group back into the system with an action plan. Instead of making a proposal for major changes and asking the congregation to support them, they implement little change cylinders in parts of the organization over which they have influence and control.

They take what is already there, rearrange it, and infuse it with grace-filled cyclical processes. Instead of just meeting as they have done before, they introduce Bible study and ask what God is inviting them to change and do at the beginning of each meeting. Instead of having a free-form discussion in which anyone who wants to speak can speak, they introduce the Mutual Invitation process as a way to include everyone's ideas. Because we are looking at the church community as a system, any little change we make with a small group will eventually affect the rest of the system.

> The way a system changes is for part of it to change. We change the part we can. Then address other parts. The controversy never really ends. Phases of it do. Pieces of it do. Some of it is addressed, but it is never completely laid to rest. In the systems approach, we handle the parts we can, knowing it will be inadequate and incomplete. When we change any of the caused factors, it is likely we will impact every part of the system.[2]

In other words, we are using a change method that is "contagious." In a book called *The Tipping Point—How Little Things Can Make a Big Difference*,[3] Malcom Gladwell documented how major change in society can happen like the spreading of an infectious disease. The idea might start with a few people, but when it is spread to a critical mass, major change will happen when the epidemic reaches the tipping point. That's what we are doing here with this process: we transmit our viruses, which are the grace-filled Christ-centered cyclical processes, to the team. This team is then planted back in their own church community with an action plan. The advantage of this model is that we can get started anywhere in the

---

[2]George Parsons and Speed B. Leas, *Understanding Your Congregation as A System* (The Alban Institute, 1993), p. 20.

[3]Malcolm Gladwell, *The Tipping Point—How Little Things Can Make a Big Difference* (Boston: Little, Brown and Company, 2000), pp. 1–15.

organization and it will infect the other parts of the organization. We start with the places where the team has power and influence. As they implement their plan, they will utilize these cyclical transformation processes. In their cyclical way, the processes can deal with rapid changes and challenges in that part of the community. Since these viruses are empowering and effective in addressing rapid changes and challenges, these cyclical processes become vital to more and more people and groups in the organization. Eventually there might be a tipping point when the community is ready for a major profound transformation.

The Process for Planned Change by itself is just another somewhat typical planning process. However, when we roll the planning process together with the cyclical grace-filled change processes, the Process for Planned Change comes alive. Like the construction of strands of DNA, the two spiraling strands—the planning process and the cyclical inclusive skills—intertwine. Theological reflection connects the two spirals like the spokes of a wheel. At its central axis is Christ. When the rearranged pieces all come together, a new dynamic form emerges, spinning out new energy and life for the community. This new DNA must first be experienced by a group of faithful members of the community. Once they start rolling into this new form, they are then planted back in their home community to effect transformational change.

If you have not been reading this book with a team of people from your community, you might want to invite a few faithful people to join you before you move on to the next part of the book. If you are in the position to do so, you can also invite teams from other churches to gather to explore change together. The implementation of the Process for Planned Change is not just a mechanical or intellectual process. It requires commitment and courage and lots of grace. Great care must be given to designing each meeting of the team(s). (See chapter 9 for a sample of a suggested meeting format.)

The Grace of the Lord Jesus Christ, the love of God, and the communion of the Holy Spirit be with all of you. (2 Corinthians 13:13)

CHAPTER 8

Sacred Acts

An Overview of the Process for Planned Change

We begin the change process by inviting a group of people to come together and commit themselves to regular meetings to study and plan in order to address the concerns of their church community. We must carefully plan the first meeting of the group. It should have the essential cyclical processes: Mutual Invitation, Bible study, and so forth. A key agenda item must be the overview of the Process for Planned Change (this chapter) and the Iceberg Analogy of Culture (chapter 4).

Right from the beginning, we make the connection between the two spirals—the planning process and the practice of the grace-filled cyclical processes. The introduction of the Iceberg Analogy will invite the group to start looking inward at their internal organizational culture. The iceberg image will also help the group to understand how the Process for Planned Change works. At the end of the first meeting, we invite those who wish to continue to commit themselves to coming to future meetings of the project. In addition to a verbal agreement, it might be helpful to invite each person in the team to sign a written covenant. (See chapter 9, Session One for a sample covenant.)[1] Once the group has agreed to commit the time and energy to this process as expressed by the outward act of signing the covenant, we are ready to move forward, or in our Cylinder image, to start rolling.

Figure 8.1
Process for Planned Change

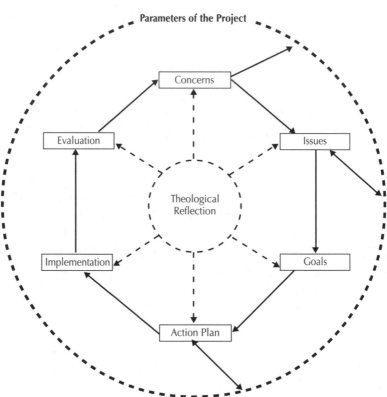

---

[1]In Law, *Inclusion,* pp. 49–57, I proposed that the first step to building an inclusive community is to covenant for time to address issues.

Theological Reflection: Inviting God to Be at the Center of Our Planning

The commitment of time to explore and plan is the first step for a group of committed people to enter the "grace margin" by stepping outside of our regular patterns, our safe zone. To maintain this grace margin, in which we are encouraged to start exploring more deeply those difficult issues that confront us, we hold up the centrality of theological reflection in everything we do involving this process. We do that by utilizing a similar format for each meeting, in which Bible study, prayers, and worship are an integral part. Every step of the way, we intentionally ask God for guidance, challenge, comfort, strength, and protection. Through every step on this journey, both inward and outward, we give thanks to God by remembering what God has done in the history of our faith community and the world. We especially remember God's saving acts through the ministry, death, and resurrection of Jesus in our celebration of the eucharist. Ultimately, it is not we who act, but God who acts through us. This is the purpose of our work toward holy change.

Parameters of the Project: Identifying the Grace Margin

The first step of our process is the drawing of the parameters. Here we ask the question, What is the boundary within which our planned change will occur? Drawing the parameters involves stretching our church community's boundaries to find the room to deal with the proposed change without pushing people into their fear zones. If we were to communicate with the church community at this time, we would need to define very clearly what we would do and what we would not do, lest some members of the community resist or even disable the change initiative. For some churches, our parameters might be an area of ministry in our church such as youth ministry, reaching out to young families, finding ways to welcome a different cultural group into our church, working out our financial problems, and so forth. For others, we might not know what the parameters are until we start collecting our church's concerns. In any case, a reflection on parameters will help us to begin identifying where the safe and fear zones of our church community are. This exploration also will initiate the work of digging into our internal organizational iceberg. As we move forward in the Process for Planned Change, we will need to revisit the parameters again.

Concerns: Approaching the Cross

Once we have done some reflection on the parameters for our potential change project, we are ready to collect concerns from our church community. Concerns are the things that we see and hear in our community—the things above the water of our organizational iceberg. What are people saying and doing? What are their feelings, yearnings, or complaints? What are some of the patterns that the church keeps on repeating? Finding out these things can be done through a survey, small group discussions, exploring the history of the church, looking at demographics of the community, and combing through past records of the church. Collecting concerns is like approaching the cross. We are outside Jerusalem looking in, observing and recording, getting ready to enter.

Issue: Facing the Cross

Once we have collected the concerns, we then discern the underlying issues behind these concerns. We look into the community's iceberg and ask, "What caused these concerns?" If concerns are like symptoms, then the issues are the disease. Very often, we move into action based on surface concerns, and as a result spend a lot of energy on tasks that never quite address the real issues. This is the most difficult part of the process. We need to assure the group that we are doing this exploration in the grace margin in which the love of God is affirmed so that people can have the courage to discuss the unspeakable. We may struggle with this for a while before being able to name the issues. Naming the issue is like facing up to the cross. It is the turning point—to name the things from which we have to die so that by dying and letting go of the old framework, myths, and assumptions, we may be resurrected with new life. We do not like the cross, but we know we must face it if we are to change faithfully.

Once we name the issues, it is important to go back and revisit the parameters. In the exploration of our issues, we might move beyond the parameters that we have set earlier. If that is the case, we need to redraw the parameters so that we can be sure that our community will be able to address the issues that we have named in the grace margin, and not in the fear zone.

Goals: Looking toward Resurrection

Once we have discerned what the issues are, we are then ready to set goals. A goal is the ideal outcome if a particular issue is addressed constructively and faithfully. The question we ask is, What would life be like if a particular issue were to be addressed constructively and effectively? If we do not state our goal clearly, we might move into doing a number of things but would never know whether we had accomplished anything. Like Jesus foretelling his Passion—in which he always included the resurrection—we too must jump ahead to look beyond Calvary and describe what resurrection looks like to us by clearly setting our goals. This is the hope and vision that will keep us going as we move through the Passion.

Action Plan: Designing the Sacred Liturgy

Once we have the goals, we are then ready to create an action plan. So far, we have been doing a lot of internal discernment and analytical work. Once we have the goal, we switch into a more practical mode, where we treat the organization more as if it were a mechanism that we need to put into action. Before we do that, it is a good idea to revisit the parameters again to make sure that, as we design our action plan, we are still staying within the parameters that we have set for our community. If we have not yet communicated clearly what the parameters of the change initiative are, the action plan itself should include helping the church community to identify the grace margin in which the action plan will be implemented. The action plan is a clearly defined (with full accountability) step-by-step plan of what needs to be done in order for the community to accomplish its goals. The action plan is like a well-thought-out liturgy. We should design it with care and prayers, making sure that each step of the action plan is blessed with the grace of God. If we are to invite our community to take up the cross and die to their old patterns and myths, we must assure them of the presence and love of God all through the journey. The action plan is the outward expression of the internal experience of grace.

Implementation: The Sacred Acts

Once we have a detailed action plan with full accountability, we are ready to put the plan into action. Having gone through the journey of discernment, and hopefully having been transformed ourselves, we are now ready to reenter our community to facilitate the liturgy that we have carefully put together. We have done the reflecting, praying, and internal exploration; now it is time to act. We embody our work, reflection, exploration, and learning by becoming the vehicle for holy change. There might have been steps that we struggled with, but we continue our work and move on. We must continue to support each other by meeting regularly to evaluate the steps that we have taken and to pray, study scripture together, and continue to actively discern God's will.

Evaluation: Celebrating the Holy Change

After we have implemented the action plan, it is important to evaluate what we have done. Here we ask, "Have we accomplished our goals? How well did we do so?" We measure the result of what we have done against the goals we have set for ourselves. In our accomplishment, we recognize the change that has taken place as a result of our sacred acts, and we celebrate that by giving thanks to each other and God. In the places where we did not do so well, we take note and learn from it. In our cyclical approach to change, there is no such thing as failure—only redemption.

The Grace-Filled Cycle Begins Again

As we reflect on the work that we have done, we will discover new concerns. The concerns might come from our observation during the implementation of our action plan. They might come from individual written evaluations of particular events that we facilitated. They will certainly surface as we evaluate the overall effectiveness of our action plan. To address these concerns, we only need to define new parameters and start a new cycle of Process for Planned Change. If we did not get to the heart of the issue the first time, we might get to it the next time. If we missed some key pieces in the first round, we will keep them in mind as we move through a new turn of the process. Each time we move through the cycle, we change what we can in the system, and we let the rest of the system react. Taking note of their reactions, we treat them as new concerns; we set new parameters and start the whole change cycle again. Each time we move through the cycle, we will move deeper into our organizational iceberg to explore deeper issues. Each time we move through it, we see ourselves more clearly and how we are not following God's call. Each time we roll around in this grace-filled cycle, we move closer to God.

Keeping this overview of the process in mind, we will now work through each step of the Process for Planned Change in the next chapter. For each step, there will be suggested activities, readings, questions for discussion, and homework.

Be sure to work through each step with a group of committed people. Take the time necessary to work through each step. I suggest that each step should take a full meeting of the group, using a similar format. Remember that this is not a linear process. Sometimes we might have to go back and revisit steps again before moving on.

CHAPTER 9

The Process for Planned Change: Step-by-Step

This chapter is organized into seven training/planning sessions, plus one final evaluation session. A team of committed members of a church community or organization can use this chapter like a workbook or a study guide. Each session is constructed with the following sections:

1. A short article on one of the steps of the Process for Planned Change. The subject of the article follows the Process for Planned Change very closely—one step per session. The planning team should read the session article before coming to the meeting.

2. Examples of the possible result of working through this step of the process.

3. A proposed agenda for the three-hour meeting to accomplish this step. This agenda can be expanded to become a longer event, or modified according to what is appropriate in the local context. Each session is organized

in a similar format, and structured like a liturgy, with prayers, songs, and Bible study. A celebration of holy communion can be added at the end of each session, if appropriate. The two changeable agenda items are the Diversity Training Segment and the Planning Segment. The Diversity Training Segment includes many cultural iceberg–digging exercises and intercultural awareness and skills. This segment is not described here because most of the activities and materials are taken from my previous books. Any new exercises and processes are described in the appendices. The Planning Segment includes a detailed process with activities to enable a planning group to accomplish the particular step of Process for Planned Change in the session.

4. When appropriate, some sessions will have additional suggested activities/processes that can help the planning team to further accomplish this step.

5. Reading assignment to prepare for the next meeting.

The Team

We recommend that you recruit/invite a group of people from your church community or organization to come to the first session, the orientation. When appropriate, you might want to invite groups from other church communities in your geographical area to the orientation meeting to explore the possibilities of working through the Process for Planned Change together. At the end of this session, those who are willing will commit themselves to five more meetings by signing a covenant. The people who signed the covenant will constitute a "team" from their church community. If more than one team commit themselves to work through the process, they can provide one another mutual support, as well as helping one another to see beyond the boundaries of their own church. If a team works through all seven sessions, the end result will be an action plan that the team can implement. After the team has finished implementing the plan, they will come together again to evaluate the result, using the suggested agenda in Session Eight.

Facilitation

It is a good idea to work with a co-facilitator to design the first session. After that, the facilitation should be shared among the team members. If you use outside facilitators, make sure that they fully understand, both practically and theologically, the Process for Planned Change as described in this book. Eventually, the facilitation of the session should be transferred to the team members, because they are the ones who will need to carry on the work in their own church community.

Orientation and Theological Reflection

What does God have to say to our planning process?

Before we start any planning process, we must invite God into the process by doing theological reflection. We are not talking about doing highly intellectual theological discourse here. Theological reflection is as simple as asking the question, What does God have to say about what we are doing? As Christian communities, our planning process is different from that of other secular organizations because of our faith. Our planning must somehow be closely connected with the core of our faith. As the team moves through the Process for Planned Change, each step must be accompanied by an active discernment of God's will. When we insist on inviting God to be part of our struggling with our issues, we maintain a place of grace in which we can be honest and open to each other and to God.

There are two ways to do this. The first is the study of scriptures at every team meeting and every gathering of the community.

> When a community studies scriptures in the grace margin, God becomes a living player in the exploration and dialogue. We do not ask, What do we want? but, What does God want? Including God in the grace margin removes the issues from a purely personal human endeavor and places them in the divine realm. It moves us beyond our need to be powerful or to be right. It turns us to God and invites us to see how God through Christ will mediate, appreciate, and even embrace our differences. (From *Inclusion: Making Room for Grace,* pp. 79–80)

The second way is to frame every meeting and gathering in the context of worship—our liturgy. For example, a three-hour meeting may begin with the singing of a hymn and with prayers, then the presentation of the Respectful Communication Guidelines, and then a short Bible study using the same Bible lesson from the upcoming Sunday worship. After that, the first topic of discussion is presented and discussed. Before or after a break, another hymn may be sung. The second topic of discussion is presented and discussed. Then there should be a recap of the decisions made and the outstanding items that will need more work. Close the meeting with a circle prayer. Sometimes it might be appropriate to celebrate holy communion at the end of the gathering. The framing of the meeting should be designed according to the worship tradition of the group.

As we begin our Process for Planned Change, we must first commit ourselves to meeting regularly, but not just to do the work of planning. Rather, we need to actively seek God's will as we move through the process. This is a covenant that we make with one another and with God to stay faithful along this journey. Think of each meeting as a time of worship: In our worship of God, we struggle with our differences, problems, paralysis, and sinfulness. We give thanks to God for the gifts, strength, courage, and grace that we have received. More importantly, we ask God to help us to be more faithful to our call to ministry and to help us turn ourselves around from our ways and learn to walk in God's way.

Example of a Team Covenant

PLANNING TEAM COVENANT

We, members of the planning team from _____
_____, commit ourselves to the three-month process of training, exploration, and action planning designed to enable us and our organization(s) to understand and plan for constructive change in order to meet the challenge of cultural, economic, gender, generational, and theological diversity today.

We will attend the training/planning sessions on the following dates:

_____ _____ _____ _____ _____ _____

At each session, we will continue to study, pray, plan, and support each other in order to arrive at a concrete action plan that will address the issues that we have discovered in this process.

Church or Ministry Group:

_____

Team Coordinator:

Name: *(please print)*_____

Address:_____

Signature:_____

Telephone:(day)_____(evening)_____

Fax:_____ E-mail: _____

Team Members:

_____   _____
Signature   Name *(please print)*

Signature	Name *(please print)*
Signature	Name *(please print)*
Signature	Name *(please print)*
Signature	Name *(please print)*
Signature	Name *(please print)*
Signature	Name *(please print)*
Signature	Name *(please print)*

Suggested Agenda for Session One

1. A Gathering Activity: singing, prayers, and so on
2. Presentation and affirmation of the Respectful Communication Guidelines. (See p. 87 of *The Bush Was Blazing But Not Consumed.*)
3. Community Bible Study using one of the lessons from the upcoming Sunday service. (See Appendix C of *The Wolf Shall Dwell with the Lamb.* You can shorten the process by using only Sections I, III–B, and IV.)
4. Training Segment:
   a. A short presentation: Iceberg Analogy of Culture (chapter 4)
   b. Activity: The Table Exercise (Appendix A)
5. Planning Segment:
   a. A short presentation: An Overview of the Process for Planned Change (chapter 8)

    b. Focus on Theological Reflection—why and how it is embedded in each planning session

    c. Explain the time commitment required for this process. Answer questions.

    d. Invite those who are willing to sign the covenant.

    e. Elect a team coordinator whose role is to communicate with team members. The coordinator is especially important when there is more than one team doing the process. Any communication that needs to go to all the teams can be sent to the coordinator and he or she will take the responsibility to pass it on to the local team.

Expected result from the planning segment of this session:

A signed covenant with at least 5 team members.

(If there are not enough people who are willing to sign the covenant, the group is not ready to move forward. Jump to agenda item 6 and end the meeting.)

  6. Prayer Circle

Invite participants to join hands in a circle. Invite each person to mentally complete the sentences:

    I thank God today…

    I ask God today…

The leader will begin by sharing her or his prayers. After she or he has shared, the leader then squeezes the hand of the person to the right. That will be the signal for the next person to share his or her prayers. If the person does not want to share, he or she can simply pass the pulse to the next person. When the pulse comes back to the leader, he or she can begin the Lord's Prayer and invite everyone to join in.

7. If appropriate, communion may be celebrated here. If not, the meeting ends here.

Reading assignment to prepare for the next session:

Inclusion, chapters 1–4
Sacred Acts, Holy Change, chapters 4 and 5

Drawing the Parameters of the Project

What are the boundaries within which the planned change can occur?

In order for members of an organization/community to support a planned change process, they must understand clearly where the boundaries are. The planning team needs to communicate clearly to the community the overall parameters of the project before engaging its members in the process. As you look at the boundaries within which you will work, you will also determine what you will *not* change.

For example, an office group reacted very negatively to the initial presentation of the planned change process. Here is a sample of their reactions:

- What are we talking about changing here?
- What if the group in this process decided that everyone should get a raise or a promotion? We can't do that.
- We're not going to change the policies of this organization, are we? That's not up to us!

After some discussion, the group determined that the purpose of the planned change process was *not* to set policy or make decisions about roles in the office. However, the process would invite everyone to focus on interpersonal relationships and team building in order to help staff members become more productive.

To help a community draw an outer parameter, we must work with the tension between stretching the boundary too far, which will push the community into the fear zone, and not stretching it far enough, being too safe. If we are too timid in drawing this outer boundary, fearing that we will push the community into the fear zone, the community may not extend its boundary far enough to allow for meaningful, constructive exploration. If we are too anxious to get things moving and push too far, the community may shut down, returning to its tightly guarded safe zone. For this process to work, we must spend a substantial amount of time negotiating this outer parameter until all the key players agree on a grace margin that is not too fearful, but not too safe. This requires gentle pushing and pulling, deliberate truth-telling, clear use of language in terms of what we will and will not do, and, most importantly, patience. (From *Inclusion: Making Room for Grace*, p. 63)

Defining the parameters will help us determine how broad or narrow our exploration should be when we move into the next step of collecting concerns. For example, a broad approach would be to ask a congregation to express their general concerns about the church. Here we are casting the net as wide as possible. This approach would be useful for a team that is just beginning to look at change without any particular focus yet. This means part of the planned change process has to do with determining the areas of concern that one can realistically address in a given time frame. A narrow approach can be, for example, asking the congregation to express their concerns about the stewardship program, the outreach program to an increasingly diverse community, the youth program, or intergroup relations within the community, and so forth.

Remember that this is not a linear process. Sometimes parameters are not set until we start collecting concerns and discerning what the real issues are. The issues that we name might push some people in the church community into their fear zone. We must then redraw the parameters to help our church community to come back into the grace margin.

The exploration in this step might result in a statement of intent for the team to take back to the congregation. More importantly, this statement should be accompanied by a set of parameters that will clarify what we will and will not do as we move through this project.

Examples of a Parameter Statement

After doing the suggested planning segment below, a team of students, faculty, and staff of a theological seminary arrived at the following parameter statement:

> The purpose of the Building Inclusive Community Project is to extend the boundaries of our common understanding toward building a seminary community that is more open to our God-given diversity.

In order to do that:

- We will create a respectful atmosphere that encourages full and honest expression and compassionate listening.
- When appropriate, we will address issues in the context of the Christian faith through studying scriptures, honoring our tradition, and praying together.
- We will seek and value input and responses from all groups in the community by scheduling all meetings during regular business hours.
- We will focus our effort on addressing issues of diversity and inclusion, and not on institutional issues that might surface but need to be addressed elsewhere.
- We will not settle on easy solutions, but acknowledge the complexity of the issues and the different perceptions that exist in our community.
- We will value the importance of inclusive process as well as achievable and measurable results.

Since the closing of the gift shop in this church in order to make room for the office of the new assistant pastor, there has been much unrest among the church members—some explicit, some behind the scenes. After some exploration of the fear and safe zones of the church, a team from the church arrives at the following parameter statement:

For our Process for Planned Change, we will invite our community to explore issues around the closing of the gift shop. As we engage ourselves in this exploration,

- We will not take sides on the issue.
- We will not just let a small group decide on the issue.
- We will consult with everyone in the parish to get their thoughts and opinions and ideas.
- We will inform all the leaders of the church at each step of our planning.
- We will explore and understand what ministries a gift shop in our church can or cannot do.

The following is a more general parameter statement from a team that did not have a focus yet but would collect concerns first and then decide on a focus later:

As the planning team invites our congregation to participate in this planning process,

- We will involve as many people in our congregation as possible.
- We will invite everyone to pray for the process to discern God's will for us.

• We will be honest in sharing our opinions.

• We will not judge each other or debate who is right or wrong.

• We will listen to each other with empathy and respect.

• We will stay within the policy of our church and our denominations.

Suggested Agenda for Session Two

1. A Gathering Activity
2. Presentation and affirmation of the Respectful Communication Guidelines
3. Community Bible Study using one of the lessons from the upcoming Sunday
4. Diversity Training Segment:
   a. A short presentation: The Concept of Grace Margin (*Inclusion,* chapter 4)
   b. Activity: Rights, Respect, and Responsibilities (*Inclusion,* Appendix B)
5. Planning Segment:
   a. A short presentation of drawing parameters on the project based on the article in this session.
   b. Invite each person to spend a period of silence to recollect an event in the life of the community that represents the community's ability to change constructively. Then recollect another event that represents the community's inability to change constructively.
   c. Invite each member to tell those stories. After each story, as a group, brainstorm on: What are the patterns, assumptions, and myths that the community considers as within its "safe zone"? What are the elements that would push the community into its "fear zone"? Who are the persons/groups that are keys to the existing

community's ability to deal with change? Record their sharing, using the following categories on a large flip chart.

SAFE ZONE:

FEAR ZONE:

KEY PERSONS/GROUPS:

d. If you were to implement the changes described in these stories again, what parameter statements would you make in order to create a grace margin for your community? Start with a fear zone item and ask: What will we not do to pull the community back from the fear zone? Couple this pulling-back movement with a pushing-out movement from the safe zone and ask: What will we do in order to address this concern faithfully? Your end result is two sets of statements that begin with: We will and we will not...Remember that you don't want to be too safe, but at the same time you don't want to push too far. Again, record the sharing, using the following categories on a large flip chart.

WE WILL...

WE WILL NOT...

e. The purpose of the above exercises is for the group to practice drawing parameters. For your planned change project you need to define broader parameters for your project by asking:
   i. What area(s) of ministry will we focus on for the planned change process? (You may also decide to not focus on any particular area yet but to use the process to explore what area of ministry you eventually will focus on. If this is the case, you need to communicate this to the community.)

ii. Given the focus of your project, explore as a team what will put the community into their fear zone, and what will be too safe.

iii. If you were to communicate with your community regarding the planned change project, what would you say to them in terms of what you would do or not do?

WE WILL...

WE WILL NOT...

iv. What steps do you need to take in order to bring the necessary persons/groups to support the potential change?

Expected result: A clearly stated focus statement, plus parameters stating what we will and will not do in this project. (Review the examples of parameters given earlier to get a better idea of what we are after.)

6. Prayer Circle
7. If appropriate, communion may be celebrated here. If not, the meeting ends here.

Reading assignment to prepare for the next session:

The Bush Was Blazing But Not Consumed, chapter 11
Inclusion, chapters 5–7

Collecting Concerns

As a member of this organization, what are your concerns?

Concerns are initial data collected from individuals and groups related to the organization. They give us an indication of what is going on in the system on a "surface" level. These are observable data above the waterline of the organization iceberg.

Concerns usually emerge as feelings, complaints, opinions, yearnings, shoulds, coulds, facts, good things that we don't do enough of, bad things that we keep on doing, and so forth. They are things relating to the dissatisfactions, satisfactions, potentials, and dreams of the people in the organization. This kind of data can be collected through the use of a survey, oral interviews, or small group discussions. Concerns can also arise out of studying the available data regarding the organization and the community in which the organization resides.

> **Caution #1:** At this initial stage of the planning process, we do not want to spend an overwhelming amount of time on collecting concerns. Some organizations spend so much time and energy on the "studying" phase that they have no energy or resources to get to the more important part of the process, which is analyzing the data and determining an action plan.

Begin with the concerns of the planning team members. If more data needs to be collected, determine a strategy and set a time limit for data collection.

> **Caution #2:** Do not judge the collected data or argue over who has the "more correct" concerns. In order for the concerns to be authentic, we must not make

111

value judgments about them, but allow differences of feelings and opinions to co-exist. Only in this way can we see a more complete picture of the organization.

The data collected do not have to be well organized or well written. We are simply interested in "a list" of statements that represent the spectrum of concerns of the organization. When we move on to discover the issues behind these concerns, we will then organize them for the purpose of analysis.

Example of Concerns

A team composed of faculty, students, and staff of a theological seminary collected the following concerns from individual interviews, surveys, and focus groups focusing on what it meant to be an inclusive community:

- We don't walk the talk.
- Institution pays more attention to resident students than to commuters.
- Some people say that we need more white men in the student body.
- The same people (students) are asked to participate in leadership.
- Don't mix God with business.
- I am non-religious; will I be shunned by those who are in the community even though I respect their beliefs? (from a staff member)
- I am not included in decisions.
- I am not appreciated.
- My ideas are ignored, not heard.
- Staff comes after students and faculty.
- How can I keep my identity while I am trying to do cross-cultural stuff as a minority?

- How can I let my sense of identity keep growing without being assimilated while I keep communicating with others who have different identities?
- Staff works hard and receives little recognition.
- The "browning" of our campus after 5.
- Some faculty won't teach evening classes, even when so many students are "evening" students.
- Faculty make assumptions and don't define their point of view.
- Policy set aside when it fits certain powerful groups' or individuals' agendas.
- No theological diversity in textbooks.
- Assumption that if you are white in the seminary you are liberal.
- Lack of respect between first- and second-career students.
- I am not in on gossip.
- This is a waste of time; you cannot change my past.
- The school is not ready for deep change.
- I feel like I am invited and shown to the last seat.
- My culture is ignored.
- I have to become white, liberal, and reformed in order to fit in.
- Spiritual expressions are very set in our traditional (European) ways.
- I never check my campus "box" and yet they keep putting important information for me there.
- Excellence emphasized without being defined in the classroom.
- I am not asked to represent the institution.
- Academic/theoretical emphasis weighs over practical and spiritual formation.
- Information not shared.

- Faculty members feel they are above everyone else. Students and faculty get all attention—like they are the only ones who make up the seminary.

A team collected the following general concerns from team members:

- How should we worship?
- If we have three services, that will break up our Sunday school.
- We are more comfortable "buying" mission work instead of doing it ourselves.
- No evangelism.
- No leadership training.
- Poor communications.
- Some say we're changing too fast. Some say we're changing too slow.
- No spiritual growth.
- Looking at the attendance records of the church for the last 10 years, we have been in a steady decline.

The team members of the church that was addressing the closing of the gift shop did some listening for two weeks and then met to summarize the concerns into the following list:

- Some people complain that they were not asked before the gift shop was closed. There are quite a few of us who volunteered for that ministry.

- It is very sad to see the gift shop reduced to just two display cases.
- Why didn't the committee that hired the new assistant pastor check out whether we have space for an office for him?
- Some people blame the senior pastor for making this decision because he doesn't like the gift shop doing secular business in his church.
- The gift shop has always given all of its earnings to the church. That's a lot of money.
- A church gift shop should only have religious items and not all the secular items that we used to sell.
- Some people are just happy that the gift shop is gone.
- Our last pastor used to be very supportive of the gift shop.
- I feel bad for the new assistant pastor. He really doesn't know what he is walking into.

Suggested Agenda for Session Three

1. A Gathering Activity
2. Presentation of the Respectful Communication Guidelines—by this session, team members should know this well enough to share their insights into these guidelines. Try the following process: *Using Mutual Invitation, invite each team member to select one letter of the Respectful Communication Guidelines and share what that particular guideline means for him or her. We will do that until all the "letters" are covered.*
3. Community Bible Study using one of the lessons from the upcoming Sunday—by this session, all the team members should be familiar with this process. It might be appropriate to invite a different team member to facilitate the Bible study each time the team gathers again.
4. Diversity Training Segment:
   a. A short presentation: Differences in Communication Styles (*The Bush Was Blazing But Not Consumed*, chapter 11)

   b. Activity: A Dialogue Process: Focusing on Differences in Communication Styles (*The Bush Was Blazing But Not Consumed,* Appendix C)
5. Planning Segment:
   a. Invite the team to complete the following three-question survey:
      i. What gifts do you bring to ____(*name of your organization*)? (Gifts can be experience, skill, talent, personality, expertise, hobby, food, equipment, time, etc.)
      ii. What concerns do you have regarding ____(*name of your organization or an area of ministry in your organization*)? (A concern can be an idea, a thought, a feeling, a complaint, a yearning, a "should," a "could," a dissatisfaction, a good thing that we don't do enough of, a bad thing that we keep on doing, something that is based on your past experience of being part of this organization, etc.)
      iii. What image or phrase would you use to describe ____(*name of your organization or an area of ministry in your organization*)? (You can draw the image if you like.)
   b. Using Mutual Invitation, invite each person to share his or her answers. Invite someone to record the sharing, using a short phrase to capture each idea.
   c. Invite the group to observe whether there are any common themes emerging out of the collected data.
   d. Decide as a group whether more concern data should be collected, before moving on to the next step. Here is a list of different ways to collect more concern data:
      i. Invite more people in the congregation to complete the same three-question survey.
      ii. Small-group discussion with pointed questions like the ones in the sample survey above. *(Notes have to be taken.)*

iii. Collect demographic information relevant to your organization. It is helpful to plot the data in graphic form.

iv. Collect organization records; for example, attendance records, financial data, membership statistics, and so forth. It is most useful if you can track a particular field of data over a period of ten to fifteen years, if not more. It is also helpful to plot the data in graphic form.

Expected result:

1. A plan to collect more concerns from the organization if needed.
2. The collected concerns should be brought to the next session.

6. Prayer Circle
7. If appropriate, communion may be celebrated here. If not, the meeting ends here.

Reading assignment to prepare for the next session:

The Wolf Shall Dwell with the Lamb, chapters 1–4
Sizing Up a Congregation for New Member Ministry, by Arlin J. Rothauge
The Life Cycle in Congregations, by Arlin J. Rothauge
(Both Rothauge booklets can be ordered through Episcopal Parish Services, P.O. Box 1321, Harrisburg, PA 17105.)

Naming the Issues

What caused these concerns?

Having collected the concerns, we need to take an analytical step to discover the issues behind the concerns. Here, we ask the question, What caused these concerns to surface? The process is like digging into the organizational iceberg to discover assumptions, patterns, and myths of the organization that might have caused the behavior above the waterline. A medical analogy may be helpful here. If concerns are seen as symptoms, the issues can be compared to the disease that causes those symptoms. Most groups are anxious to jump into solving the problems when the issues are not clearly understood or defined. If this analytical step is missing, an organization may embark on programs and strategies that may not address the heart of the concerns, resulting in wasteful use of energy and resources.

This is the most difficult part of the process. The team might need to struggle with this step for more than one session before getting the issue statements. Here are a few tests that can be used to evaluate an issue statement.

The Connective Test

Your issue statement should be connected with the concerns collected. Usually, a group of concerns might be the symptoms of one deeper issue. Ask the following question:

If the named issue is addressed constructively, will the concerns go away?

If the answer is "yes," then you've obtained a good issue statement. If "no," rework it.

The Specificity Test

Your issue will drive the goals for your project. Therefore, there needs to be some specificity to it. For example, here is a vague issue statement:

We need to increase our volunteer outreach workforce in our congregation.

This statement does not tell us why we need more volunteers. If the team sets a goal based on this issue, we could just implement any old training program. Based on the discussion, and a review of the concerns, the team discovered the deeper issue is trust. The old leaders do not trust the new younger leaders. So the team reworked the issue statement:

We need to increase the number of volunteers while building trust among the old leaders and the new.

The Neutrality Test

An issue should be stated in neutral language so that all the parties involved can agree and stay at the table to address it. Check the parameters again, so that you can name an issue in a way that will keep everyone in the grace margin. Sometimes the team might be able to name a very deep issue but decide not to write an issue statement at that level. This is because if they did, it would push the rest of the people in the community into their fear zone, where they would be not be able to entertain any idea of change. For example, a team from a deeply divided church was able to name the issue in their church among themselves this way: "There are at least two very strong, opinioned groups that are fighting with each other and with the pastor." If they had presented this issue statement to the church, these groups would simply deny it and might use their political power to disable the change process. After some more discussion, the team arrived at the following moderate issue statement in order to keep everyone in the grace margin to dialogue: "There are major differences in how people in our church understand the ministry and authority of the laity and of the pastor."

If the team decides an issue is really important to name but knows that by doing so it would cross the parameters they have set earlier, the team will need to rework the parameters again. The question to ask is, If we were to address this issue named in this manner, what do we need to say to the rest of the congregation about this change project? What will we do and not do?

Example of Issue Statements

After some discussion, the team from the theological seminary put their list of concerns into two categories:
1. Interpersonal concerns
2. Institutional iceberg concerns

The team divided itself into two. Each smaller group took their set of concerns and arrived at the following issues:

Interpersonal Issues

1. We are afraid and don't know how to engage each other with integrity and honest differences. We don't know how to live in the tension that comes from our diverse differences because we are afraid of or don't know what's on the other side.

2. There are confusions among the three different cultures at work in the seminary: academic, business, and church cultures.

Institutional Issues

1. We are in a period of transition from being a traditional theological education institution to a new educational

organization that respects and includes diversity of people and theology. We don't know how to live in this transition.

2. Demographic diversity brings with it a challenge to the perceived theological conformity required by the seminary.

3. Some students fear that the diversity initiative might require them to assimilate into the dominant culture.

The seminary has been actively addressing the issues of diversity and inclusion for more than five years, and during that time they have been utilizing some of the cyclical inclusive skills in different parts of the seminary, such as using Mutual Invitation in many classrooms and meetings. With that background, the teams were able to name deeper and systemic issues, moving the seminary toward a more profound transformation.

After a lengthy discussion, the team that was addressing their general concerns named the following issue as the key one to address first:

Many people in our church operate out of a passive, inward, self-centered culture.

The team that was dealing with the gift shop discovered a deeper issue of what the "problem" really was. The dispute over the gift shop was only a symptom of the underlying cause.

As the team explored further, they arrived at the following issue statement:

There is difficulty in communication and in understanding the relationship between the pastor's authority and the responsibilities of lay leadership in handling the affairs of the church.

They would have to go back and redo the parameter step. They might have to redraw the parameters based on this discovery and decide how to communicate the new parameters to the church community.

Suggested Agenda for Session Four

1. A Gathering Activity
2. Presentation and affirmation of the Respectful Communication Guidelines
3. Community Bible Study using one of the lessons from the upcoming Sunday
4. Diversity Training Segment:
   a. Activity: What Color Should the Church Be? (Appendix A)
   b. A short presentation: Differences in Perception of Power and their Consequences for Leadership (*The Wolf Shall Dwell with the Lamb,* chapters 2–3)
5. Planning Segment:
   a. Put all the concern data collected on flip-chart paper and post them on the wall.
   b. Invite the group to name a number of common themes emerging from these concerns.
   c. Group these concerns together by common themes.
   d. Divide the team into smaller groups. Invite each group to take one set of concerns and to discern the issue(s) behind them.
   e. Each group reports back on their issues.
   f. Put each issue statement through the three tests: Connective, Specificity, and Neutrality tests.

Expected result: Issue Statements that are connected to the concerns, specific and neutral.

If the team decides that it needs to do more work on naming the issue, create a plan to do that before the next session. Here are two more exercises that the team can facilitate in order to name the issues:

A. Working with a larger group of people from the church to explore its history, using the process in *Inclusion*, Appendix C, "Exploring the History of a Congregation." Afterward, the team gathers to name the issues that were discovered in this exercise.

B. Working with a larger group of people from the church to explore its ministry structure by using the process in *Inclusion*, Appendix D, "Is Your Church Ministry Balanced?" Afterward, the team gathers to name the issues that were discovered in exploring the ministry structure of the organization.

6. Prayer Circle.
7. If appropriate, communion may be celebrated here. If not, the meeting ends here.

Reading assignment to prepare for the next session:

The Wolf Shall Dwell with the Lamb, chapters 5–9
Sacred Acts, Holy Change, chapter 6

Setting Goals

What would life be like if a particular issue were effectively dealt with?

Having stated the issues, we can then develop goal statements. A goal statement defines the ideal anticipated outcome in relation to an issue. Most groups jump into program planning without clearly stating the ideal outcome. Developing goal statements can keep us focused on what we are trying to accomplish. Another pitfall at this stage may be that the goals are *too lofty* to be accomplished within the available time, energy, and resources.

Sometimes a goal may be *too "fuzzy,"* resulting in the inability to determine whether a goal has been accomplished or not. Here is an example of a lofty and fuzzy goal: "By Christmas, everyone in the church will be happy." This goal is not realistic, nor is it achievable, because it is impossible to make everyone happy.

Therefore, a goal must first pass the "ARM" test. We ask the question, Is this goal **A**chievable, **R**ealistic, and **M**easurable? To be more specific:

Achievable: Can it be done at all?

Realistic: Can it be done with the time, energy, and resources available?

Measurable: How will we know we have accomplished the goal?

The Connective Test

The goal must also be connected to or must directly address the issue. Check your goal statement against the issues and concerns so that you can determine whether you are still on the right track. The question to ask: If this goal is accomplished, will the issue go away? If your answer is yes, you have a good goal. If no, go back and rework it.

The Specificity Test

You goal will drive your action plan. Therefore, it must include specificity that reminds you of the issue that you are trying to address. For example, a vague goal statement sounds like this:

We will have three operating home-meeting groups by Christmas 2001.

Even though this goal statement is "ARMed," it does not give any indication of what issue the goal is attempting to address. The question is, What is the purpose of these home-meeting groups? The team reworked the goal this way after reviewing the issues and concerns again:

By Christmas 2001 we will have three operating home-meeting groups for the purpose of mutual empowerment, in order to increase leadership.

This new goal continues to focus the team on the heart of the issue, which is lack of leadership.

The Neutrality Test

The goal must continue to stay neutral. That is, it should not condition the outcome of a dispute or conflict among different groups in the community. For example, a church is dealing with the concerns raised by the proposal of a ministry project for the homeless population in the neighborhood. The proposal was put forth by a group of committed members who had done the studies necessary to support this project. Some members don't want the homeless shelter, while others support it passionately. The planning team names the issue as:

> *There are very diverse opinions, feelings, and understandings*
> *of the ministry of the church to the homeless population.*

Even though most of the team members believe the homeless shelter should continue, they do not name that as their goal. Instead, they set the following neutral goal:

> *We will help the church community to address the challenge*
> *of the homeless shelter ministry practically and spiritually*
> *and with mutual respect without conditioning the outcome.*

The phrase "without conditioning the outcome" is actually part of the parameter of the project. Since the church already knows where many of the team members stand on this homeless shelter project, the team needs to state its neutrality clearly in its goal statement.

Other Examples of Goal Statements

Continuing with the seminary team, they set the following goals to address the issues that they have named. To get the connectivity between the issues and goals, read the issues again and then read the following goals.

Put the following goals through the three tests: ARM, Connective, Specificity, and Neutrality tests.

Interpersonal goals:

1. At the end of the fall seminar next year a new class evaluation form will be designed, approved, and administered to each class to measure whether "inclusive processes" are used effectively to engage students and faculty members in rigorous discourses.

2. By September 2001 all supervisors will be trained to use appropriate skills to deal with conflict and differences, and

90 percent of staff will have experienced and learned the inclusive process.

3. By the end of the next semester year all faculty, students, and some administrative staff will have at least three opportunities to study and clarify the relationship among the three different cultures—church, education, and business—at work at the seminary.

Institutional goals:

1. For September 2001 a report created by a study group will be presented to the faculty that will include: (a) How to create educational experiences that recognize cultural/racial identity and do not assimilate or alienate the "others." (b) How to use teaching tools/experiences that recognize and affirm diversity. (c) A plan to train all faculty members to use these tools.

2. By December 2001 all faculty members will have participated in training to moderate and facilitate respectful dialogue among people with different theological/ ideological perspectives.

3. By June 2001 the seminary community will receive clear communication on the role of the minority ministry offices, especially how these offices support the various groups by helping them to keep and build their identities.

Here is the goal statement set by the team addressing the issue of spiritual formation and leadership:

By Easter 2001 we will have at least three regular groups meeting at church members' homes. The ongoing purpose of these groups is to study scriptures together and discern what God is calling us to do. By Easter each group will have declared its focus of ministry for the coming year.n

Here is the goal statement set by the team addressing the gift shop "problem." The team decided that they could stay within their initial parameters focusing on the gift shop. They set a goal that used the opportunity created by the closing of the gift shop to address the deeper issue that they had named.

To see church members communicating and the leadership working together to realize the best resolution for the gift shop issue.

Suggested Agenda for Session Five

1. A Gathering Activity
2. Affirmation of the Respectful Communication Guidelines
3. Community Bible Study using one of the lessons from the upcoming Sunday
4. Diversity Training Segment:
   a. A short presentation on the concepts of Power Analysis and Cycle of Gospel Living (*The Wolf Shall Dwell With the Lamb,* chapters 6 and 8)
   b. Invite each team member to do a power analysis on him/herself relating to different groups in the church. Having done the analysis, what does each one think the gospel calls her or him to do?
   c. Using Mutual Invitation, invite each person to share his or her insight from the reflection.

5. Planning Segment
   a. Take one issue at a time. Imagine a time in the future (6 months or a year from now) when this particular issue has been addressed constructively.
   b. What would be the measurable results? Write them down.
   c. Using Mutual Invitation, invite each person to share his or her vision.
   d. Record the information and formulate into a goal statement.
   e. Put the goal statement through the four tests: ARM, Connective, Specificity, and Neutrality tests. If it doesn't pass, go back and rewrite until it does.

Expected result: Goal statements addressing the specific issues named.

---

6. Prayer Circle
7. If appropriate, communion may be celebrated here. If not, the meeting ends here.

Reading assignment to prepare for the next session:

The Bush Was Blazing But Not Consumed, chapters 5–8

Creating an Action Plan

The action plan is a detailed, step-by-step statement of those things that must be done to attain the goals within the parameters set by the team. Before proceeding to design an action plan, the team should revisit the parameter exploration at the beginning of the planning process. The purpose is to recapture the values and norms, personal boundaries, organizational structure, and available resources within which the goals are to be achieved. The creative process requires a framework in which the vision can be realized. The stated parameters become the material with which we realize our vision. For example, a painter will get a better sense of how to realize a painting if he or she has decided on whether to paint on a stretched canvas, a wall on a three-story building, or the surface of an egg. Restating the values of the group, the available resources, the organizational structure, and the personal boundaries will give the framework within which we can realize the goals in more concrete ways.

As we put together the action plan, we will be asking team members to commit themselves to take responsibility for particular action items. Therefore, the team members need to be clear about their own boundaries and available energy and resources. The questions to ask are:

- What time commitment am I willing to give to this project?
- What gifts and resources do I bring that will help us accomplish these goals?

Sharing the answers to the above questions will enable the team to be even more realistic in creating the action plan.

Each goal should have a separate program package. Accountability is crucial in this step. Each action step should include a completion date and the name and contact information of the person(s) responsible. The written action plan should be published and distributed to the whole team. To further safeguard the accountability, an Accountable Person (AP) should be appointed. The role of the AP is to make sure that the goal is met by reminding and receiving reports from persons who have committed to do their tasks. For example, looking at the sample action plan below, the AP on September 7, 2001 (the Target Date for the recruitment of facilitators), will call Larry, who is the person responsible for this task. The AP will ask if the action has, in fact, happened. If Larry says it is done, we now have 10 potential facilitators committed to the training; the AP can just check this action step off. If Larry says that he is not able to complete the task and will need more time, the AP will inquire about how, working together, they can accomplish the task by September 14, which is the deadline.

An Example of an Action Plan

Goal Statement: By Christmas 2001 we will have at least three regular groups meeting at church members' homes. The ongoing purpose of these groups is to study scriptures together and discern what God is calling us to do. By Christmas each group will have declared a focus of its ministry for the coming year.

Accountable Person: Maria

Contact Information: phone, fax and e-mail, etc.

TARGET DATE	DEADLINE	ACTION	PERSON RESPONSIBLE
9/7/2001	9/14/01	Recruit 10 small group facilitators who will commit to being trained for the home meeting groups	Larry
9/15	9/22	Facilitator training program designed	Larry, Maria, Juan & Ming
9/29	10/5	All training material ready	Ming
10/6	10/6	A day-long training for facilitators. Three facilitating team forms and covenants signed	Team
10/21	10/21	Help church members understand the purpose of the home meeting groups, invite them to sign up with one of the groups, and commissioning of the facilitators during Sunday service.	Pastor Tom
		After church, facilitators meet with possible groups to provide an experience for church members to understand what these meetings are like. Written evaluations.	Facilitators
11/4	11/4	Meeting of facilitators to review evaluation and to plan the first session	Juan & Larry
11/11	11/11	Small groups will start monthly meetings	Facilitators
12/9	12/9	Facilitators meeting to design the next four meetings leading up to Easter	Juan & Maria
Dec. 01–March 02		Monthly meeting of small groups	Facilitators
3/17/02	3/17	Meeting with Pastor Tom to work in time for small groups to share their ministry focus in the Easter Service	Larry
3/31	3/31	Easter Service in which each small group shares its ministry focus with the church community	
4/8	4/8	Evaluation meeting	Ming & Larry

Suggested Agenda for Session Six

1. A Gathering Activity
2. Affirmation of the Respectful Communication Guidelines
3. Community Bible Study using one of the lessons from the upcoming Sunday
4. Diversity Training Segment:
   a. Have two team members prepare ahead of time to read the short play *Band-Aid* (Appendix C).
   b. Using Mutual Invitation, invite each member to share their reflections, answering the discussion questions for *Band-Aid*.
   c. A short presentation on Ethnocentric Response to Difference (*The Bush Was Blazing But Not Consumed*, chapters 7–8). Ask the team members if they can identify which response the two characters were coming from in the play *Band-Aid*.
   d. Recap program strategies for persons in different stages of their intercultural sensitivities.
5. Planning Segment
   a. Hang a long piece of paper on the wall or lay it on a long table. (A good way to do this is to tape two pieces of flip-chart paper together.)
   b. Draw a line across the length of the paper. Put today's date on one end and the date of the completion of the goal on the other end. This will be the time line for the action plan. (See Figure 9.1.)

Figure 9.1

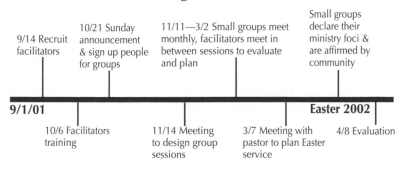

c. Ask the group the following question:

In order for us to accomplish the goal on this date, what needs to happen between today and the completion day?

d. Each team member is invited to contribute by adding on to the time line things that need to be done and when they should be accomplished along this time line. If this is the first action plan for this team, make the plan as detailed as possible. If there are many activities that need to be done in a certain period of time, that probably means that the time frame for the action plan may not be realistic. The team might need to find a new completion date and spread the tasks out a little.

e. After the team has agreed that all the tasks that need to be done are on the time line, invite a recorder to fill in the Action-Plan Table similar to the example given in this session. Individuals are invited to take responsibility to make sure each action item will be completed on time. The "Deadline Date" is the day when that action item must be completed. The "Target Date" should be at least three to seven days before the "Deadline Date." The reason for this is that the Accountable Person for this goal will contact the person responsible for this action item on the "target date." If the task is not done, the person committed to this action item still has a few more days to complete it. If the person responsible knows at the target date that he or she will not have time to complete the task, the Accountable Person can help find other persons to fill in to complete the necessary task.

f. If there are action items that nobody wants to take on, this means the action plan again is not realistic. The team then needs to go back to the time line and readjust.

g. Each goal should have an action plan table completely filled out. For each action plan, there should be an Accountable Person. Make sure there is an evaluation action item at the end of the action plan. The action plan table should be copied and distributed to everyone in the group.

h. The Accountable Person (AP) will use the action plan table as a guide and contact the appropriate person at the appropriate time to inquire about and support the work and to ensure that the necessary tasks are completed.

Expected result: A fully accountable action plan table for each goal.

6. Prayer Circle
7. If appropriate, communion may be celebrated here. If not, the meeting ends here.

Reading assignment to prepare for the next session:

The Wolf Shall Dwell with the Lamb, chapters 10–11
The Bush Was Blazing But Not Consumed, chapters 9–13
Inclusion, chapters 8–10

Sending the Team Forth to Implement the Action Plan

Once we have the detailed action plan, we are ready to implement the program. It is important for the planning team members to come together again to finalize the action plan, to decide how we can support each other during the implementation period, and to pray and ask God for support and guidance. At this point, it is important to check again the necessary steps taken to help the church community stay in the grace margin by communicating clearly what the parameters are and to ensure that each action item that we implement is within these parameters. We also need to check whether everyone involved has enough resources and support to fulfill their commitment. Review the grace-filled cyclical processes and skills learned throughout this planning process. We need to be intentional in how we apply these skills and processes as we implement the tasks of the Action Plan.

The Accountable Person must act with a balance of demanding accountability and providing support and encouragement. Don't forget to have fun while doing the job.

Suggested Agenda for Session Seven

1. A Gathering Activity
2. Affirmation of the Respectful Communication Guidelines
3. Community Bible Study using one of the lessons from the upcoming Sunday
4. Diversity Training Segment:
   a. Review all the material from the training segments in the last six sessions. Give team members time to reflect on their personal learning.
   b. Using Mutual Invitation, invite each member to share the significant learning that he or she has gained.
5. Planning Segment

a. As a group, write down a list of processes and skills that would be helpful for the implementation of the action plan. These skills include:

- Presentation and Discussion of the Respectful Communication Guidelines
- Mutual Invitation
- Community Bible Study
- Circle Prayer
- How to adjust to High and Low Context styles of communication
- Iceberg Analogy
- Repeated Meeting Format
- And so forth

b. Discuss how these processes and skills can be used for the various tasks of the action plan. Are there places in the action plan that we need to modify or make more specific?

c. Using Mutual Invitation, invite each person to share her or his reflection on the following question:
What physical, environmental, spiritual, and emotional conditions do I need in order to implement my part of the action plan? What resources and support do I need?

d. Based on the sharing, determine the ways in which the team members can support each other during the implementation period.

Expected result: To gain a clearer sense of how to implement the action plan and how the team members can continue to support each other.

6. Prayer Circle
7. If appropriate, communion may be celebrated here. If not, the meeting ends here.

Evaluation

Have we accomplished what we set out to do?

When the action plan is completed, it is vital to conduct an overall evaluation of the project against the goal statements. For teams that facilitated events and activities as part of their action plans, written evaluations collected at these events and groups will be very helpful.

Here is a list of typical evaluation questions:

1. To what degree have we accomplished our goals?
2. With what are we dissatisfied?
3. With what are we satisfied?
4. What were the new concerns that surfaced as we implemented our action plan?
5. Did we work within the parameters that we had set? Were these parameters too safe, resulting in little change? Or were these parameters stretching too far, pushing people into their fear zone?

It is quite likely that the evaluation step will evoke new data that can then be treated as concerns and a new *process for planned change* can be instituted for another round of exploring and planning. Draw up a new covenant with new meeting dates. Invite a team of people to commit themselves to the new Process for Planned Change.

Suggested Agenda for Session Eight

1. A Gathering Activity
2. Affirmation of the Respectful Communication Guidelines
3. Community Bible Study using one of the lessons from the upcoming Sunday

4. Invite each team member to review all the evaluation material collected during the implementation period. Give them time to consider answering the following questions:
   a. To what degree have we accomplished our goals?
   b. With what are we dissatisfied?
   c. With what are we satisfied?
   d. What were the new concerns that surfaced as we implemented our action plan?
   e. Did we work within the parameters that we had set? Were these parameters too safe, resulting in little change? Or were these parameters stretching too far, pushing people into their fear zones?
5. Using Mutual Invitation, invite each team member to share the accomplishments and satisfactions first.
6. Using Mutual Invitation, invite each team member to share the dissatisfaction, concerns, and so forth.
7. Based on the sharing, as a team, compile a list of learning from the experience of implementing the action plan.
8. Invite each team member to reflect on the following questions:
   Is there a need for starting another Process for Planned Change?
   If yes, what would be the parameters?
   Who should be on the new planning team?
9. If a new Process for Planned Change is appropriate, elect a team coordinator who will gather a group of potential team members to start the process again.
10. Prayer Circle
11. If appropriate, communion may be celebrated here. If not, the meeting ends here.

The Table Exercise

An experience to explore our internal cultural iceberg

Objective: To help participants better understand the concept of exploring their internal cultural icebergs

Type of Group: Adults

Size of Group: 6–15

Setting: Participants should sit in a circle.

Materials: Copies of the worksheet—one per participant

An image of an iceberg—on a flip chart, overhead projector, or handout

Time Required: Depends on the size of the group. A good way to determine how much time is needed is to multiply the number of participants by five minutes.

How to Proceed:

1. If the group has not affirmed the Respectful Communication Guidelines, present them now and invite participants to commit to following them for the rest of the session.

2. If the group has not had a chance to discuss the Iceberg Analogy of Culture (chapter 5), do a short presentation before this exercise. Another way to do this is to invite participants to read chapter 5 before coming to the session and invite them to share their insights about the chapter before this exercise.

3. To ensure safety in the exercise, present the following additional ground rule:

   When you are invited to do something that you don't want to do or are not ready to do, just say "pass." When we are exploring our icebergs, sometimes we find ourselves in places that we do not want to deal with in this context. That's okay. Just stop. We invite you to take care of yourself and not step beyond the boundaries that you are not willing to cross.

4. Invite everyone to affirm the additional ground rule.

5. Hand out the worksheet for this exercise. Invite participants to picture themselves when they were young, maybe ten or twelve years old. Ask them to recall a scene during a mealtime on an ordinary day. Give them the following questions:

   a. What was the shape of the table at which you ate? Draw it. If you did not eat at the table, describe how you ate.

   b. Who was involved in this scene? What were they doing or saying?

   c. How did you feel? What did you do?

6. Give participants some time to write or draw their reflection.

7. Invite them to consider the following exploratory questions:

In what ways has this experience of eating affected your perception of:

a. power and authority?

b. male and female roles?

c. hospitality?

8. Give participants time to reflect and write on this question and to work through the rest of the worksheet.

9. Using Mutual Invitation, invite each person to share his or her insights from this exercise. Remind them that they can pass if they do not want to say anything.

10. Summarize learning from the exercise, and be sure to include the following:

In this exercise, we took something that we could see, hear, taste, and touch—the part of our cultural iceberg that is above the water—like the table at which we ate, and we dug into the internal part under the water. We asked what we might have learned from this experience. What values, beliefs, attitudes, assumptions, patterns, and myths did we learn from this experience? In this exploration, we might discover things that we have not thought of before. But these things might still be affecting us now.

Our church organization/community is also like an iceberg. There is the part that we can see and articulate readily—the part above the water. However, a large part is under the water—the internal organizational culture. These are the patterns, myths, and assumptions that are hidden and can be very hard to articulate. When we are trying to enable our church community to change, we will have to discover the things that are in the internal organizational iceberg of the church. Not until we can discover and let go of the framework of our old paradigm that has caused our inability to respond to God's call to ministry in the world today will we be able to embrace the new, more faithful possibilities for ministry. In the Process for Planned Change, when we are collecting the concerns of our church community, we are observing and recording the things that we can see, hear, and touch in our community—the external culture. When we are discerning the issues behind the concerns, we are exploring our internal organizational iceberg.

Problems to Anticipate:

Sometimes this exercise can bring out very strong emotions from reviewing past negative experiences. Reassure the participants that they can share as much or as little as they wish. They can pass altogether, and no one will pressure them to share at a level that they are not willing to reveal. Invite participants also to be respectful of each other's boundaries.

The Table Exercise Worksheet

Picture yourself when you were young (maybe ten or twelve). Recall a scene during mealtime on an ordinary day.

OBSERVATION

What was the shape of the table at which you ate? Draw it.

Who was involved in this scene? What were they doing or saying?

How did you feel? What did you do?

EXPLORATION

In what ways has the experience of eating at a table of this particular shape affected your perception of:

1. power and authority?

2. male/female roles?

3. hospitality?

CLARIFICATION

What did you learn from investigating this experience?

1. explicitly?

2. implicitly?

What values, beliefs, attitudes, and assumptions about others did this experience instill in you?

What Color Should the Church Be?

A role play to explore differences in perception of power and self-identity

Objective:	To help participants to understand the injustice created by differences in perception of power, personal identity, and communication styles
Type of Group:	Adults
Size of Group:	At least nine people
Setting:	Participants should sit in a circle. Inside the circle, set up nine chairs for the role players.
Materials:	Copies of the nine role descriptions, three green name tags
Time Required:	Fifteen minutes for the role-playing; thirty minutes for debriefing and discussion

145

How to Proceed:

1. The facilitator gives the following explanation and purpose of the role play:

   The purpose of the role play is to learn about some of the assumptions that we might have regarding power, identity, and communication. By playing a role, you are invited to behave differently from your "normal" mode of behavior. This may lead to a better understanding of yourselves and others. This role-play exercise is called "What Color Should the Church Be?" It involves a group of nine people in a meeting trying to decide what color they should paint the exterior of the church. I would like to have nine volunteers. If you are used to volunteering, this is a particularly good role play for you to participate in. I also want to invite especially those who were educated in the United States to be part of this role-playing experience.

2. Once you have nine volunteers, the facilitator gives out the nine printed role instructions to the players. Be sure to ask the three "Wednesday Group" players to put on the green name tags. Also, the facilitator should remind the players to:

   Imagine how you would behave if you were this person as described in the role instruction. Also, if in your instructions, you have a boldfaced paragraph, please make sure you follow that instruction as you play your role.

3. While the players are reading their roles, the facilitator gives the following explanation to the observers:

   While our players are preparing for their roles, I will explain the situation to you, the observers. St. _____ on the Edge is a church at the edge of a changing neighborhood. It has suffered a consistent decline in the last ten years. To make up the budget shortfall, the congregation rents out the church building to a local community group to use every Wednesday night. They don't know what exactly the Wednesday night group does, but there are always a lot of people showing up at their gathering. Last Sunday the pastor announced to the congregation that the church received a donation for the purpose of painting the exterior of the church building. The church has been beige for as long as the church members can remember. However, over time, the exterior of the church has become dirty and run-down and is now in need of a new paint job. The condition associated with the donation is that if the money is not spent by Wednesday of that week, it will disappear.

The pastor said, "I have set up a meeting on Tuesday evening for anyone who is interested in helping us decide what color we should paint the church." A number of people volunteered. The players who have no name tags are the ones who volunteered from the church. "Furthermore," the pastor continued, "since the Wednesday group has been using the church for over a year now, I have invited a few members from that community to come as well. We will try to be as inclusive as possible in this matter." They are the three people with green name tags. The pastor then added that he would not be there but had appointed a chairperson to run the meeting.

It is now Tuesday evening, only two days after the initial announcement on Sunday.

4. Ask the role players if they have any questions about their roles. If there is no question, let the role playing begin.

5. Allow the role play to go on for at least fifteen minutes. After some substantial interactions have taken place (e.g., the Wednesday Night group being ignored, individual challenges, power plays by the church members,

negotiations on the color, etc.), the facilitator can end the role playing.

6. Keeping the role players in their positions, the facilitator asks the following questions to debrief the group.

To the observers:

a. What did you observe about the interaction of the group? (Invite a number of different observations regarding both the church members and the Wednesday Night group.)

b. Can you speculate on what might have caused the different characters to behave the way they did? Besides what their role instructions asked them to do, what might be the values, beliefs, and assumptions behind their behaviors?

To the chairperson:

c. What were you instructed to do, and how successful did you think you were in accomplishing it? What techniques did you use to help the group to be more inclusive? What techniques worked and what didn't? Why?

To the church members:

d. What were your goals when you entered this meeting? (Many will say that their purpose was to convince others that their color was the right color for the church.)

e. As a person in your role, how did you feel about the Wednesday Night people initially? Did your feeling toward them change over the course of the meeting? How?

f. I want you to read your role instructions again. Except for the "Beige" role, which has specific instructions on how she/he is to behave, were you told to push for your color in the instruction? (The answer is no.)

g. The facilitator gives the following reflection:

> Most of you jumped to the assumption that if you have a belief, you are to push for it and convince others that you are correct. This assumption is not universal. In many different cultures, when people have a belief or strong preference, they may not come right out and push for their ideas. Only in the United States and a few other countries is this considered "normal." The other assumptions that you made were that you can speak whenever you like without being invited and that you speak on behalf of yourself. Is that correct? (Note: sometimes you will have a player who behaves naturally in a high-power distance non competitive way. If that happens, point out the behavior and ask that player to share what might be behind his or her behavior.)

TO THE WEDNESDAY NIGHT GROUP:

h. [Ask one of the Wednesday Night group players to read the role instruction. Point out the differences in assumptions—that is, they were instructed to talk only when the leader invited them to speak, and they were a group-oriented bunch of people.]

i. As a person in that role, how did you feel initially at this meeting? How did you feel about the church members?

j. Over the course of the meeting, did your feeling about yourself and the church members change? How?

k. What did you learn as a result of playing this role?

TO THE WHOLE GATHERING:

l. What did you learn about yourself in this role-playing exercise? What did you learn about your assumptions and perceptions of personal power and your self-identity?

m. How have these assumptions caused you, in the past, to be in conflict with others who do not hold the same assumptions, consciously and unconsciously?

7. De-role the players by asking them to imagine putting their roles back into the instructions. Collect the name tags and instructions. Send the players back to their seats.

8. Follow the role play with a short presentation on Power Distance and the "wolf and lamb" scenario. (*The Wolf Shall Dwell with the Lamb*, chapters 2–3.)

9. Reemphasize the importance of using Mutual Invitation as an essential skill to intervene in the "wolf and lamb" scenario.

Problems to Anticipate:

Be careful not to give the Wednesday Night Person role to a person of color. Playing this role might bring up too many negative memories and can be counterproductive. You can get more understanding from giving this role to a historically dominant person, because this person will have an opportunity to understand what being shut out feels like.

Sometimes, a Wednesday Night Person player might break out of his or her role and start talking without being invited. During the debriefing, ask how the other Wednesday Night Persons felt about one of them not behaving as the role called for. This sharing might lead to more in-depth understanding of how sometimes a token minority representative might be forced to give his or her individual opinions in order to get into the discussion and be counted. But by doing so, that person might have a problem returning to his or her community because he or she did not properly represent the community.

Sometimes, a role player might insist that the role description did ask him or her to enter the meeting to push for his or her color. This is only true for the Beige role. For the others, simply invite her or him to reread the role and look for specific instructions for that. Point out that having a belief does not necessarily mean that one has to convince others about that belief as well. In our North American upbringing, we are conditioned to jump from having a belief to having to push for getting what we want. The assumption is not universal, but a North American cultural pattern.

Role Descriptions: What Color Should the Church Be?

1. CHAIR

You were asked by the pastor of the church to chair a meeting to decide what color the church building should be. An announcement had been made last Sunday about this meeting. Also, the pastor has invited representatives from the group that uses the building on Wednesday night. (You recognize them by their green name tags.) Your job as the chair of the committee is to make sure everyone is included in this meeting and to help the group make a decision by the end of the meeting.

2. BEIGE

You heard about a meeting on the color of the church building, so you decided to go, because you believe that the building should stay the same color as before—beige. You have never seen the church any color other than beige. If the church is changed, you will feel you have lost your church, and you will stop pledging. You give $5,000 dollars a year to the church.

3. GREEN

You heard about a meeting on the color of the church building, so you decided to go, because you believe that the building should be green. Green is the color of a leaf and represents growth for you. You think the church should be a place where people can grow spiritually.

4. WHITE

You heard about a meeting on the color of the church building, so you decided to go, because you believe that the building should be white. White represents cleanliness. You think your neighborhood is going "downhill," because the streets are getting dirtier every day. A clean white church will send a message to others to keep the neighborhood clean.

5. WHITE

You heard about a meeting on the color of the church building, so you decided to go, because you believe that the building should be white. White is the color of purity. You like the idea of a "pure" church, because there is so much impurity in the world today. Also, your favorite holiday is Easter, and the color of Easter is also white.

6. BLUE

You heard about a meeting on the color of the church building, so you decided to go, because you believe that the building should be blue. Blue is the color of the sky, and the church building should look like it is part of nature.

7. WEDNESDAY NIGHT PERSON #1

You are invited to attend a meeting to decide what color the church building should be. You and the other two people with green name tags are representing a community of people who use the church building every Wednesday. You do not have an opinion on the color of the building, but you know your community does. But the meeting was called on such short notice that you have not had a chance to have a community meeting on the subject. You don't even have a chance to talk with the other two people with green name tags about what color your community would like. You do not feel comfortable about giving your personal opinion about the color because you do not believe that would represent your community's wish.

Also, in your community, you are taught to speak only when you are invited to speak by the leader of the group.

8. WEDNESDAY NIGHT PERSON #2

You are invited to attend a meeting to decide what color the church building should be. You and the other two people with green name tags are representing a community of people who use the church building every Wednesday. You do not have an opinion on the color of the building, but you know your community does. But the meeting was called on such short notice that you have not had a chance to have a community meeting on the subject. You don't even have a chance to talk with the other two people with green name tags about what color your community would like. You do not feel comfortable about giving your personal opinion about the color because you do not believe that would represent your community's wish.

Also, in your community, you are taught to speak only when you are invited to speak by the leader of the group.

9. WEDNESDAY NIGHT PERSON #3

You are invited to attend a meeting to decide what color the church building should be. You and the other two people with green name tags are representing a community of people who use the church building every Wednesday. You do not have an opinion on the color of the building, but you know your community does. But the meeting was called on such short notice that you have not had a chance to have a community meeting on the subject. You don't even have a chance to talk with the other two people with green name tags about what color your community would like. You do not feel comfortable about giving your personal opinion about the color because you do not believe that would represent your community's wish.

Also, in your community, you are taught to speak only when you are invited to speak by the leader of the group.

Band-Aid

A short play dealing with intercultural sensitivity

Objective:	To enable participants to understand better the different levels of intercultural sensitivity and their consequences in interracial relationships
Type of Group:	Adults
Size of Group:	Any
Setting:	Participants should sit in circles of six people.
Materials:	Two copies of the play *Band-Aid,* by Eric H. F. Law
	Copies of discussion questions—one per group
	A "flesh"-colored Band-Aid as a prop for the play

Time Required: Fifteen minutes for the reading/
performance of the play, and 30–45
minutes for the small group discussion

Preparation: Invite two actors/participants to rehearse
the play ahead of time. Experienced
actors can actually perform the play.
With inexperienced participants, a
reading of the play is sufficient.

How to Proceed:

1. Explain the purpose of performing/reading the play.

2. Set up the scene by reading the stage directions at the
   beginning of the play.

3. Performance/reading of the play

4. Give participants time to reflect, in silence, on the following
   questions:
   a. How did you feel about the two characters? Did you
      find yourself being empathetic to either one of the
      characters? Did the characters say things that you have
      said yourself before?
   b. What were the woman's solutions to interracial issues?
   c. Why didn't her solutions work for the man? What was
      causing the man to become more and more irritated
      and angry as the play progressed?
   d. What was the man's perspective on interracial issues?
   e. If a "Band-Aid" is not a helpful image to address
      interracial issues, what would be a positive image that
      we can use?

5. If the Respectful Communication Guidelines have not
   been presented and affirmed, review them now and invite
   everyone to commit themselves to following them for
   the sharing.

6. If the participants are not already in groups of six people, move them into groups now.

7. Using Mutual Invitation, invite each person to share her or his reflection on the questions.

8. Re-gather the large group. Follow with a presentation of the ethnocentric and ethnorelative stages of intercultural sensitivity (*The Bush Was Blazing But Not Consumed,* chapters 7–8). Ask the participants to reflect on these questions:
   a. In what stage in this intercultural sensitivity development was the woman in the play?
   b. In what stage was the man in the play?
   c. Invite each group to share their alternative images for dealing with interracial concerns that were shared in the groups.

9. Close the session by refocusing the participants on the programmatic strategies for each stage. (*The Bush Was Blazing But Not Consumed,* chapters 7–8.) Invite participants to think about where in these developmental stages the majority of their church community members are regarding a particular group—e.g., a different ethnic/racial group, women, gay/lesbian/transgender/transsexual groups, persons with disabilities, and so forth. Connect the alternative images that they shared with the ethnorelative stages, if appropriate. Emphasize that we do not move through these stages just once in our lifetimes. We might have to go through them each time we meet a new group of people who are different. If we do not know anything about the differing group, we might have to start from the beginning again and move slowly through all the stages.

Problems to Anticipate:

Some people might have a problem with the term "ethnorelative," fearing that if everything were relative, then there would no morality. For example, someone might challenge this term or idea with the "culture" of Hitler. They would ask, "How can that culture be neither good nor bad, but just different?" Here is how I would respond to that:

> When we use the term ethnorelative, we are not using it in the political or international relations arena, as in dealing with Hitler. That requires another kind of analysis. We are using the term in the context of interpersonal relationships. Basically, we use it to describe how we react when we meet someone who is different. Do you react to someone who is different ethnocentrically by saying the difference does not exist, or that the difference is to be defended against or minimized? Or do you react to someone who is different ethnorelatively by accepting, adapting, and integrating his or her worldview?

In any case, do not spend too much time on the presentation of the ethnocentric and ethnorelative stages. Give just enough information and then refer the participants to the two chapters in *The Bush Was Blazing But Not Consumed* if they have any more questions.

Band-Aid

A Play by Eric H. F. Law

(Los Angeles. One year after the 1992 riot. It is break time at an interracial harmony conference. MAN OF COLOR is in the hallway outside the auditorium. He is dabbing a white napkin on his forehead. WHITE WOMAN enters.)

WHITE WOMAN: Wasn't that wonderful? Those kids were so cute and talented!

MAN OF COLOR: Excuse me?

WHITE WOMAN: I love the costumes and the drums. I mean, I never knew Koreans had drums.

MAN OF COLOR: I'm...

WHITE WOMAN: I always believe there are a lot of commonalities between Koreans and African Americans. If only we had done more of these kinds of events, we wouldn't have had the riot...

MAN OF COLOR: I'm sorry, I...

WHITE WOMAN: I mean, "civil unrest" a year ago. Don't you think so?

MAN OF COLOR: I'm not in the mood to talk!

WHITE WOMAN: I beg your pardon?

MAN OF COLOR: Go talk to someone else!

WHITE WOMAN: Are you not feeling well?

MAN OF COLOR: No, I just...

WHITE WOMAN: (Notices the bloodstain on his white napkin.) You're bleeding!

MAN OF COLOR: It's nothing.

WHITE WOMAN: Let me take a look.

MAN OF COLOR: It's really...

WHITE WOMAN: Oh, you have a cut. Let me see what I have. (She searches through her pocketbook and pulls out a first-aid kit.)

MAN OF COLOR: You always carry a first-aid kit with you?

WHITE WOMAN: Earthquake preparation. You never know when the Big One is going to hit. (She opens the kit and looks for a Band-Aid.) What happened?

MAN OF COLOR: The TV camera.

WHITE WOMAN: TV camera?

MAN OF COLOR: It attacked me.

WHITE WOMAN: You're very creative.

MAN OF COLOR: I was sitting next to the camera and someone tripped over the cable and the camera landed on my head.

WHITE WOMAN: Let me put this on. (She puts the Band-Aid on his cut.) There.

MAN OF COLOR: (He turns and looks into the mirror.) You wouldn't have one of those clear Band-Aids, would you?

WHITE WOMAN: What's wrong with…?

MAN OF COLOR: No, it's just…

WHITE WOMAN: Men have come a long way, I tell you.

MAN OF COLOR: I beg your pardon?

WHITE WOMAN: Ten years ago, no man would have cared about how he looked with a Band-Aid on his face.

MAN OF COLOR: I'm not…

WHITE WOMAN: Back then, a Band-Aid was just a Band-Aid.

MAN OF COLOR: I don't mean…

WHITE WOMAN: You don't have to explain. I guess women's liberation has liberated men, too.

MAN OF COLOR: It has nothing to do with…

WHITE WOMAN: You can care about the way you look. That's all right with me.

MAN OF COLOR: It's not all right.

WHITE WOMAN: It's all right. You can…

MAN OF COLOR: This Band-Aid doesn't match my skin! I

thought I never would have to wear one of these so-called "flesh-colored" Band-Aids again when they came out with the clear ones.

WHITE WOMAN: Too bad. It'll have to do for now. Just be a good boy and…

MAN OF COLOR: Don't call me boy!

WHITE WOMAN: (Silence.) I'm sorry. I didn't mean to…

MAN OF COLOR: I'm sorry. I overreacted.

WHITE WOMAN: So.

MAN OF COLOR: So.

WHITE WOMAN: How do you like the program so far?

MAN OF COLOR: I don't want to talk about it.

WHITE WOMAN: Come on. I want to hear what you think.

MAN OF COLOR: I'm only here because my university sponsors this thing.

WHITE WOMAN: I'm on the planning committee. If we did something wrong…

MAN OF COLOR: I don't…

WHITE WOMAN: You've got to tell us so we can…

MAN OF COLOR: Why is the burden always on us!?

WHITE WOMAN: Burden?!

MAN OF COLOR: Why is it always our responsibility to teach you? Why can't you figure it out by yourselves?

WHITE WOMAN: All I wanted was your reaction to the program! What's wrong with you?

MAN OF COLOR: Of course, there is always something wrong with people of color.

WHITE WOMAN: I didn't…

MAN OF COLOR: It's always our fault, isn't it?

WHITE WOMAN: I think you have a problem with your anger.

MAN OF COLOR: I think you have a problem dealing with people of color.

WHITE WOMAN: This is an interracial harmony conference.

MAN OF COLOR: You think having Korean dancers and tacos and gospel choirs is going to create interracial harmony?

WHITE WOMAN: We're supposed to find common ground. Why dwell on things that divide...?

MAN OF COLOR: You just don't get it, do you?

WHITE WOMAN: Get what?

MAN OF COLOR: You're white, and I'm a person of color.

WHITE WOMAN: Why is everything "racial" to you?

MAN OF COLOR: Because they are!

WHITE WOMAN: No, they're not. We're both human beings. Can we start from there?

MAN OF COLOR: When you say, "We're all human beings," aren't you saying I should be like you?

WHITE WOMAN: No, I...

MAN OF COLOR: Then what do you mean?

WHITE WOMAN: It means exactly that—we are all human beings. If we respect each other, we'll be able to live together in harmony.

MAN OF COLOR: Of course, but there's a price to pay.

WHITE WOMAN: Of course, nothing comes easily.

MAN OF COLOR: I mean for people of color.

WHITE WOMAN: You're thinking "racial" again.

MAN OF COLOR: I have to. If I don't, I'll get hurt.

WHITE WOMAN: Get hurt by whom?!

MAN OF COLOR: You. No, I don't mean you. I mean people like...You know what I mean.

WHITE WOMAN: No, I don't know what you mean!

MAN OF COLOR: I used to think I was just like everybody else. Then one day I noticed I had been in the same job for too long and all the whites with fewer credentials and less experience just passed right by me. I thought maybe I wasn't doing my job right. Then I talked to other people of color; and they said the same thing. So

WHITE WOMAN: how should I think? Was it race or was it my incompetence? Either way, I lose. That's what hurts.

WHITE WOMAN: I can understand that.

MAN OF COLOR: How can you under—

WHITE WOMAN: That's no different from growing up as a woman in a male-dominated society.

MAN OF COLOR: No, it...

WHITE WOMAN: As a woman, I have to watch every step I take. Every corner I turn, I may be attacked by powerful men. And I don't mean just physically. Women have to fight every step of the way to get to where we are.

MAN OF COLOR: Yeah, when you fight, you win.

WHITE WOMAN: We've made some progress.

MAN OF COLOR: When people of color fight back, we get killed.

WHITE WOMAN: That's not...

MAN OF COLOR: Martin Luther King.

WHITE WOMAN: Yeah, but...

MAN OF COLOR: Malcolm X.

WHITE WOMAN: But you have made great strides.

MAN OF COLOR: We changed a few laws; that's about it. What good are the laws when you can't get justice, even with solid proof, like a videotape!?

WHITE WOMAN: That's over. Can't we move on?

MAN OF COLOR: It may be over for you. For me, it's a...

WHITE WOMAN: Look at you—a person of color working in a prestigious university *(looks at his badge)* as the director of the Multicultural Center. Thirty years ago, this could not have happened.

MAN OF COLOR: Thirty years ago, there was no multi-cultural anything.

WHITE WOMAN: You should be proud.

MAN OF COLOR: Yeah, but...

WHITE WOMAN: If there were more educated people like you, we wouldn't be dealing with this racial stuff. I really believe that education is the solution.

MAN OF COLOR: May I remind you that you are dealing with racial stuff, even with educated me.

WHITE WOMAN: Yeah, but I can talk to you.

MAN OF COLOR: You mean you can't talk to other people of color with fewer degrees, with less-expensive clothes, with less of the proper English language?

WHITE WOMAN: All I'm saying is that you're educated, you've made it, and you're a great example of...

MAN OF COLOR: All we've got are pigeonhole jobs. It's politically correct to have a person of color as the director of the Multicultural Center.

WHITE WOMAN: That's not true.

MAN OF COLOR: Yeah, they'll keep a couple of people of color on the list for every job opening, but it's who gets the job that counts. In the kind of jobs that we get, you can't move up and you don't want to move down; so the only move is out.

WHITE WOMAN: Then fight back!

MAN OF COLOR: It's easy for you to say.

WHITE WOMAN: Take the university to court!

MAN OF COLOR: You just don't get it, do you?

WHITE WOMAN: What don't I get this time?

MAN OF COLOR: You're thinking like a white person.

WHITE WOMAN: Just what does that mean?

MAN OF COLOR: You white people all think alike.

WHITE WOMAN: You're being...

MAN OF COLOR: It's true. You're all racists and don't even know it.

WHITE WOMAN: Not all whites are...

MAN OF COLOR: Have you read the history of North America?

WHITE WOMAN: It's not fair to those of us who really tried to...

MAN OF COLOR: Who murdered the Native American Indians and stole their land? Who kidnapped Africans and forced them to be slaves? Who locked up the Chinese on Angel Island? Who put the Japanese Americans in concentration camps?

WHITE WOMAN: I don't have to take responsibility for what white people did in the past!

MAN OF COLOR: If you enjoy the privileges of being white, then you should take the re—

WHITE WOMAN: Privileges?

MAN OF COLOR: Like you can take the university to court and believe you can have a fair chance of winning! You can count on the color of your skin not to work against you when you apply for a loan. You can go into the store and buy flesh-colored Band-Aids that match your skin!

WHITE WOMAN: For your information, my father marched in Selma with Martin Luther King. I was taught to be in solidarity with the poor and the minorities from the time I was a child. I made a conscious decision to give up our power and work in the ghettos. I live in South Central.

MAN OF COLOR: So?

WHITE WOMAN: I have given up my privileges to be in solidarity with you.

MAN OF COLOR; That doesn't mean...

WHITE WOMAN; So how can you dismiss me as "just another white"?

MAN OF COLOR: What do you want from me?

WHITE WOMAN: I'm not one of them!

MAN OF COLOR: What do you want from me?

WHITE WOMAN: I'm not a racist!

MAN OF COLOR: Look. I think the decisions that you made are very courageous. But you can't expect me to give you a medal for what you have done, or what your father did.

WHITE WOMAN: I can't believe…

MAN OF COLOR: What about my parents' and my grandparents' suffering? What you did because of your guilt doesn't even begin to compare.

WHITE WOMAN: We've got to start some-

MAN OF COLOR: You might choose to live in South Central today. But tomorrow, if you choose, you can move back to your lily-white neighborhood. You have a choice. That's why you're white, and I'm a person of color.

WHITE WOMAN: *(She covers her eyes with her hands.)* Deal with me.

MAN OF COLOR: What are you doing?

WHITE WOMAN: Deal with me, I can't see.

MAN OF COLOR: This is exactly the problem I have with people like you!

WHITE WOMAN: Deal with me.

MAN OF COLOR: You're not blind!

WHITE WOMAN: I can't see the color of your…

MAN OF COLOR: You're just pretending to be blind!

WHITE WOMAN: Why won't you deal with me when I don't care about your skin color? *(Silence.)* Deal with me! Deal with me!

MAN OF COLOR: You see this Band-Aid?

WHITE WOMAN: *(She uncovers her eyes.)* Band-Aid!

MAN OF COLOR: All my effort of trying to make it in this country is like putting on this Band-Aid—

one at a time. You see, when we get hurt in your world, we put on a white Band-Aid. The next time we get hurt, we put on another one, and another one, and another one. Pretty soon we are covered with Band-Aids. Then one day, you look in the mirror and you suddenly see how ridiculous you look. So I painfully peeled these Band-Aids off one at a time, revealing all the old wounds. They never healed. This interracial harmony conference, affirmative action, busing, and my damn job are nothing but Band-Aids. *(He peels off the Band-Aid and hands it to her.)* But, no thanks; I'd rather bleed.

———   THE END   ———